"A wonderfully helpful book about the tender graces and gritty practices that will keep your relationship not just alive but beautifully thriving."

—Daphne Rose Kingma, author of
True Love, Finding True Love, and *The Future of Love*

"Judy Ford is fast becoming my favorite inspirational writer. I am touched, uplifted and best of all, feel differently about life. She speaks for love in a way that moves me closer to who I really am. Find out for yourself the hidden wisdom in this deceptively simple book."

—Jay Schlechter, PhD, author of
Intimate Friends: An Antidote to Loneliness

"Heartfelt, honed, and honest, *Every Day Love* is written by an authentic romantic who also happens to be a renowned family therapist and prolific author of best-selling 'inner guidebooks.' Her latest book is a must-read for anyone seriously interested in loving and being loved. What you can discover within these pages will stay with you and inspire you in all of your relationships. Who wrote the book of love? Judy Ford. And it is finally here!"

—Antonia Rojas Kabakov, choreographer and teacher

EVERY
DAY
LOVE

EVERY DAY LOVE

THE DELICATE ART OF CARING FOR EACH OTHER

JUDY FORD

Published in the United States by Viva Editions, an imprint of Cleis Press Inc., 2246 Sixth St., Berkeley, CA 94701.

Printed in the United States.
Cover design: Scott Idleman
Cover illustrations: iStockphoto.com
Text design: Frank Wiedemann
Cleis logo art: Juana Alicia
First edition
10 9 8 7 6 5 4 3 2 1

ISBN: 978-1-57344-413-2

Library of Congress Cataloging-in-Publication Data

Ford, Judy, 1944-
 Every day love : the delicate art of caring for each other / Judy Ford. -- 1st ed.
    p. cm.
 ISBN 978-1-57344-413-2 (trade paper : alk. paper)
 1. Love. 2. Interpersonal relations. I. Title.
 BF575.L8F57 2010
 158.2--dc22
                                    2010020787

Love anything and your heart will be wrung and possibly broken. If you want to make sure of keeping it intact you must give it to no one, not even an animal. Wrap it carefully round with hobbies and little luxuries; avoid all entanglements. Lock it up safe in the casket or coffin of your selfishness. But in that casket, safe, dark, motionless, airless, it will change. It will not be broken; it will become unbreakable, impenetrable, irredeemable. To love is to be vulnerable.

—C. S. Lewis

TABLE OF CONTENTS

A SPECIAL KNACK

This book is about exactly what the title suggests, everyday love, love that keeps us going. Behind the scenes of our active public lives there is an unseen thread connecting us and challenging us to remember to be loving. Everyday love may not be as glamorous as romances portrayed on the big screen, may not be as perfect as we aspire to attain, but it is steady. Everyday love feels comfortable and yet it is more than a feeling—it is the combination of attitudes and actions that satisfies, supports, and sustains. It is the love that shapes us into who we are becoming.

Folks in the know, the well married and a wide range of experts, report that daily love is complicated and requires a special knack. Articles, movies, books, magazines, advice columns, and scientific research report that couples don't understand each other. With all the admonitions that loving each other is not for the faint-hearted or weak-minded, we tremble and wonder if we're up to the task.

How do you love a man who squeezes the toothpaste in the middle when you would prefer it neatly pushed from the end? How do you love a man who exaggerates the good deal he negotiated on his car? Can you really love a man who decides that attending church is not necessary for spiritual development, when you're committed to teaching Sunday School? How do you love a man who reads great literature and is well versed in current events when you're stuck on tabloids and soap operas? And what about the man who can't articulate his feelings? Is it possible to be in tune with a man who says, "You worry too much," when you try to talk with him about your girlfriend's dramas?

How do you love a woman who insists that you talk to her, buy her flowers, and read her mind? Can a man love a woman who disapproves of motorcycles when he is planning to trade in the one he already owns for a bigger one? What about loving a woman who insists on no television in the bedroom when he can't fall asleep without it on? Can a man love a woman who insists on eating organic greens and veggies when he's a steak-and-potatoes kind of guy? How do you love a woman who is begging for another baby when you think two is enough? Is it possible to love each other when the differences feel like slivers festering under the skin?

It seems to me that there's a conspiracy of silence about what tears couples and families apart and about the work that goes on behind relationship doors to repair it. The subject is a closely guarded secret. People are very tight-lipped about the day-to-day interactions that chip away at love and what tiny gestures keep love thriving. I've been studying love relationships for over 25 years, and while I don't claim to have the final word, I can testify to the fact that we all still have much to learn about the nitty-gritty of this delicate art. Falling in love is easy, but daily love turns out to be harder than expected.

Every Day Love, a peek into love that comforts and flourishes, is filled with couples' stories and experiences that are often overlooked as insignificant. Presented in these stories are the nuts and bolts of day-to-day relationships. Chock full of tales of lovers' quarrels, heartaches, and healing gestures, this book gives you snapshot views of the *loving nuances* that transform our misunderstandings. Here are small yet noteworthy actions that keep love fresh. *Every Day Love* is brimming with universal expectations and disappointments, along with tips for nurturing and mending love. Reading these tales is both fascinating and instructive. At a certain point, you'll probably rub your eyes amazed that people like you (normal people!) actually do these things. Maybe you'll slap your forehead and say, "Hey, what's going on?" Novels, plays, poetry, and musicals have been written about these scenarios; they probably will be again. These are the perennial dramas.

The delicate art of everyday love is not about changing or coercing your sweetheart into doing the things you want; rather it's about becoming the best partner and ultimately the best person you can be. What can you learn from reading *Every Day Love*? To avoid the pitfalls and celebrate the differences. After all, wasn't it curiosity about those differences that piqued our interest in the first place? It's the delicate pinch of difference that adds the tang, the spice, the va-va-voom that keeps us fascinating and fascinated. We all are different, for sure, and we're similar too. We all yearn deeply to love and be loved. And so, with longing in tow, the fine-tuning begins.

To all of you, the many clients who generously told me your stories and gave me permission to share them in this book, thank you from the bottom of my heart for all you have taught me. I have changed your names to respect and honor your privacy. Your stories will touch many lives.

To Antonia and Joel Kabalov, Jay Schlechter, Brenda Knight, Mark Rhynsburger, and the believers at Viva Editions, I am grateful for your brilliant collaborations.

Here's to Love in all its forms,
Judy

NOTHING IS GUARANTEED

You might outgrow your partner. You might separate.

You may end up broken-hearted. Your lover may leave.

You may leave your lover.

However, if what you are doing now isn't enhancing personal growth and relationships and if you keep reacting in the familiar old pattern, then it is almost certain that nothing will change.

You will stay stuck.

Whereas if you change one tiny response, if you take an honest look at what you are doing to contribute to the predicament you find yourself struggling with, something within you is bound to blossom.

Chances are, you will grow.
You may become empowered.
You might even see more clearly what your next step could be.

You will have to decide if examination is worth the risk.
Is it worth the hard work to expand, evolve, and understand yourself better? Is it worth the effort to become the best person and partner that you can be?

You will have to choose.
Will you take a chance on love?

BEST OF THE BEST

If you've ever awakened in the middle of the night and felt the warmth and comfort of your partner next to you, if you've ever walked through the front door with hopeful anticipation that your loved ones are home, if you've felt a quiet exhilaration as your sweetheart greeted you with a smile, if you've ever been tied up in knots with worry or stress and felt it melt away in your sweetheart's reassuring presence, you know the deep satisfaction of day-to-day love.

Everyday love feels like home—it is home, a safe haven, a respite from doubts and demands, pulls and pressures. The spot where you let down, drop pretending, toss off your mask, lay down your armor, and are accepted as you are— blossoms, thorns, and all. That indefinable resting place where you feel most like yourself and where you gather unconditional support that inspires personal growth. It is everyday love that props you up, provides assurance that you are lovable, ignites faith that good things are coming, gives you another chance when you've messed up, offers hope when you've lost belief in yourself, and extends a cushion to rest upon when you're weary. It is the safety net that keeps you from falling through the cracks. Without such a backup it is difficult to believe in yourself; without daily love it is as if you don't have a friend in the world.

Everyday love feels good, and yet it is more than a feeling: it is the combination of attitudes and actions that satisfies, supports, and sustains. As wonderful as it is, it can be unpleasant. As exciting as it might be, it will be frustrating too. It is definitely not all whoop-tee-do. The delicate art takes graceful skill even when we don't feel like putting in the effort. You will have to be attentive, disciplined, daring, intuitive, heroic, trustworthy, imaginative, and honest. You will have to labor and work night and day to hone it. Everyday love is knowing everything about your sweetheart and wanting to be with him or her anyway.

LOVE LESSON

1. Be daring. Dwell in possibility. Consider: Is it possible to love? Answer: Yes. Consider: Is it possible to love every single day? Answer: Yes. Yes. Yes.

2. Be disciplined. Maintain a loving perspective. Speak about what is going right six times as often as you speak about what is going wrong. For everything that goes wrong, something goes right. Things go wrong, but more goes right.

3. Be heroic. Some people maintain that troubles come in threes and are defeated by those troubles. Heroes overcome troubles by creating a way out. Instead of counting difficulties, count solutions. Instead of counting defeats, count blessings. Instead of expecting what you want, generate what you want. Instead of complaining about your partner, be heroic, be a loving role model, and become the person you would like to be.

4. Be attentive. Notice how the simple solace of a roof overhead, food on the table, and imperfect good souls gathered around is enough of a spark to keep going. Everyday love provides the backing to keep on keeping on, motivates us to do better, makes us believe that we can.

5. Be intuitive. Listen to the little voice within. It is a power source that transmits the wisdom to manage your life.

LOVERS AND SEEKERS

You've made an essential step. You've turned the page and are still reading. I take that to mean that you've committed to love and with that pledge you've joined the world of lovers and seekers. Seekers who love love and are faithful to the journey, excited about discovery, unwavering in their pursuit. We are all beginners. Like lovers and seekers everywhere, our enthusiasm about joining such a group is tempered with angst and bewilderment. You've probably experienced already that daily love is not all whoop-tee-do. But there is another side to it.

- Just as there are warning labels on all kinds of consumer products and fine print on every contract, the delicate art comes with warnings and fine print too. Before we proceed, I feel obligated to point out what the warnings are and what the fine print says. That way, if you want to opt out, you can do so with minimal damage.

- It is easy to be loving when the setting is romantic, when you've got extra jingle in your pocket, when you're looking good and feeling fine, but when one of you is out of sorts, exhausted, overwhelmed, and distracted, behaving lovingly requires conscious effort. It's in those moments of restlessness and upheaval that you find out who you are and what it truly means to love each and every day.

❀ Love matures and changes as we mature and change. We change for love and love changes us. The qualities that make a loving partner are the same qualities that make a loving person.

❀ Brain scientists tell us that being in love is like being high on cocaine. On the other hand, behaving lovingly is downright demanding. While falling in love is beyond our control—powered by pheromones and dopamine—behaving lovingly is a choice that requires concentration, awareness, effort, and goodwill.

❀ We fall in love with a person who has the qualities that we would like to develop in ourselves. We see all the budding possibilities and are excited to be accepted by such a wonderful and perfect person. Watch out! A strange fog will cloud your vision and you will become disoriented; rather than developing the qualities in yourself that you would like, you will try to develop the other person's potential. This creates havoc because there is only one person's potential that you can develop, and that is your own.

🌸 It's not that you won't have problems in your love relationships, it's that you will. You definitely will.

Before you give up, let me encourage you to keep your heart open and hang in there. You know what they say: When the going gets tough, the tough get going. When the daily grind seems impossible, lovers keep loving and seekers keep seeking. The ways of love are very unpredictable. Sometimes people yearn for love and look for it, and sometimes they simply fall in love without even looking. But whether they've yearned for it or just fallen into it, lovers know that love feels wonderful. That's something you don't need to be told.

LOVE LESSON

1. Opt out. You don't have to be a lover or seeker. No one is forcing you. This is your choice. If you would rather avoid the trouble altogether and become a curmudgeon, that is your right. Don't worry about it. The true lovers will try to love you anyway.

2. Bear witness. When you accept your new identity, celebrate and make an announcement: "I am a lover and a seeker." Nothing to be ashamed about here.

3. Be optimistic. Lovers and seekers are the eternal optimists. Politicians, money-changers, and fighters may poke fun at your choice, but they can't help it—they're pessimistic.

4. Be brave. Courage is going ahead even when you are afraid. "Love is scary," a seeker told me, "because I have to let go of a part of myself to let love in. My mind gets in the way and I shut down to protect myself. I am afraid of being hurt."

5. Hang out with seekers. On your journey you will need support from other lovers and seekers. Form a group, check in with each other, hold discussions on topics related to the delicate art of caring.

IN THE BEGINNING

From the euphoric twinges of a new romance to the comforting reassurances of fingers entwined and hearts connected, our longing for love is universal. We need love. All of us. Men, women, children, poets, mathematicians, philosophers, politicians, bankers, teachers and students, mechanics and ministers, farmers and marketers, poor and rich, we all crave love. From the moment we are born until the moment we die, we all are seekers. Even sourpusses, who say they no longer believe in love, hope to find it. We want it all: kissing and conversation, appreciation and understanding, compassion and caring, connection and cuddling, romance and passion. Everyone everywhere yearns for the potential love promises.

Falling in love is easy, sustaining love more difficult. You were in love. You made a commitment, moved in together, perhaps exchanged vows. You love your partner yet sometimes you don't feel it. You wonder if you are still in love. What happened? On the heels of blissful promises and everlasting pledges, confusion and heartache commence. We commit, and suddenly there's more anguish than expected. Are we deluded? Does the intoxicating mystery of not knowing the other turn sour by knowing too much? Still the heart does not give up.

And so, dear reader, the very first question we must ask

is: If everyone wants love, needs love, desires love, looks for love, searches for love, crosses fingers and prays to find love, and if everyone knows that in the end love is all that matters, why, then, is day-to-day love so difficult?

LOVE LESSON

1. Buy a journal. Not just any journal but a journal with a beautiful cover and unlined paper.

2. Designate a half hour of private time each day to read *Every Day Love* and write in your journal.

3. On the first page of your journal write your name. On the following pages list all the people—platonic and romantic—that you love now and all the people that you loved in the past. Paste in their pictures.

4. On a separate page write this question: Why is love so difficult? Answer by writing a sentence or paragraph about each of your past and present loves. Make a list of difficulties you've faced or are facing now. Again include platonic and romantic loves.

5. Close your eyes and take a deep breath. Say this and write it: "Daily love is hard work, and I am worth it."

DEATH AND THE QUEST

I've been actively studying love since Jack, my first husband, died suddenly of a heart attack when we were both 29 years old. His death forced me to stop and pay attention. I'd deluded myself into believing that Jack and I would grow old together. I'd been lazy, assuming that love—in the form of the man of my dreams—would be enough. I was duped into thinking that I was safe and that my course in life was set. I believed there was plenty of time for loving.

Death is harsh. When Jack walked through the double doors of the emergency room, when he lay on a gurney behind a torn gray curtain, when he took his last breath, it seemed that love died with him. With the doctor's matter-of-fact delivery, "Sorry, we did everything," and then "Would you like to see the body?" a void walked in and made a home in my soul. Desperate and in despair, I could not cry. My love was gone. Mercifully, the fog of grief came quickly and brought occasional, momentary relief. I was a young widow and it was acceptable to be sad. Friends and strangers who heard my story felt genuinely sorry, but what could they do? How cruel fate is. I never questioned "Why me?" out loud, but I sensed its rumblings. For a year or more, I walked through days with wide-open wounds.

When you're in a wounded condition, suffering from lack of love, you do have choices: you can kill yourself, distract yourself, question everything you thought you knew. I considered suicide for a moment, but the fundamentalist religion I'd been raised in had left a permanent imprint. Suicide would mean I'd burn in hell for eternity. Besides, I could renege and use that option later if need be. First, I would search for answers. What is love? Where do I find it? How do I keep it?

If you are disheartened about your relationship or discouraged about love, you do have options. If you haven't yet started considering love, I invite you to join me. Make a pledge to study love. You might begin as I did, by reading Erich Fromm's classic book *The Art of Loving*. His ideas rearranged my thinking. I took a closer look at myself, my beliefs and judgments. It was as if Jack's premature death jump-started my search. Is love available for everyone? Is love the answer to our human condition? How do I recognize love? Will I ever love again?

I apologize if talking about death is a downer, but since I didn't make up the rules it's really not my fault. The reality is that we all face death. Death is coming. I have worked in a hospital emergency room and in an intensive care unit. I've held hands with the dying and stood by as family members absorbed the news and wailed. Do you know what happens in those last days and last hours? A great deal of hand-holding and whispering goes around the room accompanied with limitless "I love you"s and tears. I have sat in the corner when death was near and love was palpable.

"Love is the only satisfying answer to the problem of human existence," Fromm wrote.

LOVE LESSON

1. Begin a quest. Postpone suicide, addiction, and all forms of self-destruction. Instead make love your quest. Question everything you think you know about love and learn everything you can.

2. Be open-minded. Read books on the subject, such as *The Art of Loving* by Erich Fromm.

3. Take death into account. Death is one subject that shakes up the status quo. Have you experienced the death of a loved one? Didn't it shake you up? Didn't you focus a little more on what matters most after that?

4. Reflect on death. A relationship is not a panacea for all angst. No one escapes death's clutches.

5. Practice saying "I love you" out loud. Say it out loud right now. Look in the mirror and say it again. Say "I love you" to everyone you think you might love.

SLIPPING AWAY

We are all slipping away. The reader of this book will die, and so will the writer. Imagine that. Imagine saying goodbye to everyone you know and everyone who contributed to your well-being. Just focusing on those tender connections makes you want to pick up the phone and tell those persons how much they mean to you. That is why I bring up this sensitive subject. If we remember that death is coming, perhaps we will remember to open our hearts. Perhaps we won't wait for a perfect moment or the right person. We won't postpone love until the chores are done, until we're rested, or until we're safe with enough money in the bank. We won't relegate love to the back burner. We will be generous, less stingy with our smiles and our hugs, we'll lend a helping hand. Perhaps we will open our arms and spread love all over the place.

When I talk with clients I ask, How would you rate yourself in the love department? Are you satisfied with how loving you behave toward your sweetheart, your children, your parents, your friends, your neighbors, strangers, and the planet? Or could you do better? And what about loving yourself? Do you love yourself?

The vast majority of folks give themselves poor marks. Everyone—except young children—acknowledges that they could do better. I asked a seven-year-old boy how he would rate himself and he answered, "Good, but my mom and dad don't love each other as much." When I shared his observation with the parents, they had to agree that their seven-year-old was better at loving than they were. Based on my professional and personal experience, I believe we are all born with the capacity to love. Sadly, our capacity weakens if we don't develop it, practice it, use it. If we value fame and fortune, power and possessions, more than we value love, eventually we forget what matters most and lose it. In the love department, we are all out of shape and we need to shape up. We are all beginners.

LOVE LESSON

1. Give yourself a love rating from 1 to 10 (10 = the highest). What rating have you earned?

2. Think of the most loving person you know. What is it about them that makes you feel loved when you are around them?

3. If you were to die today, what would your loved ones say about you?

4. Write down the names of all the people you have loved, the names of those you love right now, and the names of all the people you would like to love. If you don't know their real names, give them a nickname. Send a love thought their way. For example: "May love surround my cousin Jane," "May love surround Grandma Rita." Since love is not only meant for the people you love, name the people who might benefit from uplifting thoughts and send loving vibes their way too.

5. Let's remember that our bodies are slipping away. Let's not let love slip away in the process.

STUDY. PRACTICE. MEDITATE.

"If you want flat abs, Judy," my trainer insists, "you must go to the gym." She says that wishing for flat abs will not produce results. To be in shape and toned you have to be dedicated. You have to work hard and sweat. She tells me that going to the gym is not enough either. It turns out I also have to eat more veggies, cut down on sugars, lift weights, and do aerobics. She advises me to hang out with people with similar intentions so that when I get discouraged they will spur me on.

"If you want to be a writer," my mentor advises, "you have to write." The difference between a writer and a wannabe is that a writer writes even when she isn't inspired. After I have formed my thoughts and experiences into sentences and paragraphs, my editor marks up my pages and suddenly writing becomes rewriting. "Drop the clichés and go deeper," she urges.

Proficiency in the arts or sciences requires consistent devotion and it is not always smooth sailing. Becoming adept, developing talents, and honing skills requires study, practice, concentration, meditation, and stick-to-itiveness. It is the same with being a lover. Musicians learn the scales long before they play with the symphony, mathematicians memorize basic rules before they progress to complicated formulas. In the same way, relationships require subtle and complex responses, so we all have considerable skills to master. Lovers are not happy 100 percent of the time; as a lover you must be emotionally brave. A true lover never gives up. A true lover aims not to find love or have love, but to *be love*.

LOVE LESSON

1. Dedicate yourself. You are not powerless. Love is not like a lottery prize, bestowed on only a few random individuals. If you desire love-filled days you must be dedicated to lifelong study.

2. Meditate. Meditating on love daily changes your talk, your actions, and your mood. Meditation is clearing your mind so your heart remains open. A love meditation is not about finding love but rather being love. Go through the day with the mantra "I am love."

3. Commit to daily practice. Experts start as beginners. There are no shortcuts. To keep on track, read about love and write favorite quotes in your journal.

4. Surround yourself with lovers. There are haters and there are lovers. "I recognize love when I see it," a student told me, "and I recognize it when I don't and I feel sad." That is why he no longer watches the news. Learn to recognize the difference between love and not love. Surround yourself with love news.

5. Let sadness arise. When you begin the study of love you may feel sad because it sometimes seems as if you've been cheated out of your share. There may be days when love seems unattainable. Sadness comes with love and can teach you compassion.

PARTICIPATE IN CHANGE

Throughout this book you will find 72 love lessons. These little assignments are change agents with potential to freshen your day, revamp your outlook, and update your attitude. If you complete at least half of the assignments, chances are that you will gain a new perspective about the principles of love, and that alone will restore enthusiasm for creating the best relationship possible. I have been assigning these lessons to clients for years, and a significant number tell me that they end up feeling more tender and behaving more tenderly. Within these assignments lie opportunities for bringing out the best in you and for seeing your partner with renewed appreciation.

May I suggest, dear reader, that if you find yourself resisting these assignments, stop for a moment and ask what your objection is. Perhaps the assignment seems too elementary, too obvious, or downright silly. But look at it this way: most of the assignments take only a few minutes. They are meant to bring awareness to truths that you probably already know but have been overlooking. If you really don't want to do one of the lessons, skip to the next one.

Every interaction between you and your sweetheart is an opportunity for more intimacy (*in-to-me-see*). For example, if your sweetheart is feeling pushed into doing something that she has no intention of doing, this is an opportunity for you say, "No problem, honey, I just thought we might have fun with it." If on the other hand you are the one stubbornly refusing, it may be worthwhile to look honestly at why such a little thing brings out your mulish side. If your automatic reaction is to dig your heels in yet again, consider reexamining your position. Stubbornness is the wet blanket on collaboration. When you find yourself resisting and realize you have no good reason to resist, think about this: If what I'm doing isn't bringing the closeness I desire, perhaps trying a new way will.

LOVE LESSON

1. Think outside the box. These assignments are like little guideposts pointing in the direction of creating an innovative love alliance.

2. Search for the kernel of insight. Experiment. Do each lesson in a spirit of inquiry. Use the lesson to propel the two of you in a direction that you haven't explored before.

3. Win–Win. The lessons are not meant to indicate success or failure. There are no right or wrong answers, no grades, and no scorekeeper. The lessons are invitations to infuse the day with new enthusiasm.

4. Write lessons for each other. If you don't understand or like the lesson I've written, the two of you might write your own. It will be fun to see what the two of you want the other to learn. Send your lesson to judy@judyford.com and I will share it with others.

5. Stay the course. Do not let discouragement take hold. If you don't like where you are today, tell yourself this: Where I am today will not be where I end up.

BE A STUDENT

My dictionary says love is "a strong affection or a strong attachment to a beloved person," but I think love is much more than that. Love is suddenly seeing someone or something as so extraordinary, so precious, so lovely that you think you're going to burst—whether it's a child, a lover, a sunrise, or the scent of a rose. When you love, you know that love is a miracle. No one has to tell you.

Love is a mystery. Perhaps relationships can be understood, but love is unexplainable. I've noticed that even when I give a little love to a complete stranger, someone I know I will never meet again, a thrill suddenly goes all through me and I am filled with joy, bursting with it. Can anyone explain that? Can anyone explain why giving a little love to a stranger should feel so wonderful? Someone from whom you will never receive anything? I think that is part of the immense mystery of love. In a way, love has nothing to do with anyone else. It's the quality of our heart, an inner state of being. In a way, we are love, and that's why we're so delighted when we're allowed to show it.

I sometimes think we use the world *love* too loosely. We say we love our car, our computer, our boat, and of course we are happy to have all the little goodies we get and we "love" whoever gives them to us. But none of that has anything to do with love. When you love someone, you love that person just for being who they are, not for what they can do for you. Perhaps they've never done anything for you, perhaps they never will, but somehow that doesn't matter because you love that person anyway. Isn't that strange? When I took a college course in economics, I learned that all of economic theory was based on the idea that everybody was selfishly looking out for their own interest. But I don't think that's true. I think we're taught to be selfish, we're taught we should be selfish, but actually we are very loving beings who often simply don't know how to express love. There are so many taboos on love that most of the time we just don't know what to do with it, and that drives us a little crazy.

Someone once said, "If you love your children, you go dancing to your office." To me, love is the mystery that allows us to hold our head up higher, to whistle while we work, to sing, to giggle, melt, and soften. Love is transforming. Love makes us young again, and if you are young, it makes you eternal. In fact, looked at through the eyes of a lover, love doesn't even exist—there is only the immense thrill of YOU.

LOVE LESSON

1. Accept the invitation. Love invites you on a journey to discover all things love, not what you think love should be, but what love is and can be.

2. Define love. Can you try? Begin by listing 20 words that you associate with the feeling you have when your heart is open. Ask your partner to participate and perhaps together you'll end up with a sonnet.

3. Treat yourself better. How many times have you heard it said that to love others you have to love yourself? Not so easy, is it? How do you treat yourself? Do you mutter put-downs about yourself? Or do you whisper, "It's okay, little darling, you're doing the very best you can and that is enough for me." Start with that and see where it takes you.

4. Know that you are lovable. What do you think you deserve? What you think you deserve is probably what you will get. Love is the unexpected miracle available to everyone.

5. Let love define you. What matters in this lifetime is how well you love. Love is an art form. Let loving be your label. When someone asks what you do, answer: "I'm a student of love."

CHAPTER II

A LIFELONG STUDY

The delicate art of caring for each other
is a lifelong study, a course in opening your senses
and softening your spirit.

The art of loving is a simultaneous process of loving
oneself while loving another. The capacity to overcome fears, release insecurities, sort through issues,
act with compassion and integrity—these are skills
you will need to excel in this graceful art.

To be loved by a person who also loves him or
herself is the highest rung on the ladder.

PUPPY LOVE

If you've ever spotted a puppy and brought it home, you know the exhilaration that comes with falling in love. A cute wiggly puppy stares at you from its cage, and you're smitten. This most special one-of-a-kind adorable puppy chooses you. Seems meant to be, and you're hooked. You adopt puppy and take it home. Perhaps you buy a fluffy bed and a stylish collar. After all, nothing, absolutely nothing, is too good for this lively bundle. You're ready and willing, and you're thinking, How hard could it be? You tell yourself, It won't be much trouble.

Turns out puppy will be trouble. While bringing puppy home is thrilling, scooping poop is not. Turns out puppy is a demanding little fellow. A demanding fellow with needs—needs that don't match up with your own. You want to sleep but puppy loudly whimpers. You want to eat your dinner in peace but puppy begs for bites. Your friend comes over and puppy jumps on her new dress. Puppy barks at the mailman, pees on the carpet, and chews your shoes. Puppy needs exercise. You feel guilty if you don't get up early to take puppy for a walk. No more meeting friends after work, because puppy needs another walk. Puppy gets very lonely. Puppy needs company, so you sign puppy up and pay for doggy day care. Puppy needs manners too, so off to obedience classes you go.

Yes, indeedy. Love is more than feeling good and being swept away. Love is a commitment to doing things you aren't inclined to be doing. Love is learning things you never thought of learning. Love is putting your own needs aside for the sake of a puppy. Soon puppy grows up and life gets back to normal: You're busy. You're tired. You're preoccupied.

You don't like to admit it, but there are days when you can't remember exactly why you fell in love with puppy in the first place. In fact, on an hour-to-hour basis it's nearly impossible to remember any kind of thrill at all. Your plate is full. You're easily distracted. You're trying hard, striving to get ahead, attempting to fit in, your mind is reeling, hoping for appreciation, feeling guilty because you're not good enough, twisting yourself into being something you are not but thinking that you should be, doing the acceptable thing, paying the bills, pretending you don't care when you're heart is shattered, pretending you don't have feelings, being stoic, sitting in traffic, watching the stock market, watching the computer, seeking entertainment, shuffling schedules, bettering yourself, working at a job that pays the bills but doesn't feed your soul—it is no wonder that there is no time for hanging out with puppy.

The puppy grows up and you barely notice—how quickly the months and years go by. You love your dog but there's less inclination to show it. That's the downside. The upside is that your dog always notices you. Your dog is ever faithful. Always wagging his tail. Isn't your sweetie a little like that too? Ever faithful, always available, waiting patiently for you to notice.

LOVE LESSON

1. Prepare for trouble. Puppies and sweethearts are trouble, that's for sure. There might even be days when you wonder, What was I thinking? Those thoughts are natural.

2. Meet their needs. All God's creatures got needs. Needs for food and shelter, exercise, a little entertainment, and big doses of affection. Teach him or her a trick or two. Puppies and sweethearts are creative too. Dogs learn tricks, like fetching, herding sheep, and leading the blind all over town. What tricks can your sweetie do?

3. Think on the upside. Day-to-day love is complicated and a hell of a lot of trouble. But there is the upside, too. There is someone waiting and happy when you come home.

4. Make amends. Fess up: lately you've taken your sweetie for granted. Don't berate yourself—after all, you've got a lot on your plate. You've been doing the best you can, but even so, you can make it up.

5. Walk. Isn't this fun? Try not to complain in front of your dog or in front of your sweetie. Grab the leash, grab a hand, and take them for a walk.

COULD THIS BE YOU?

When they were first married they talked and made love all night. They hope to again, but, well, they have reasons why they don't. Like many couples with three children under the age of 10, Alice and James are busy. Their plates are full.

James is an ambitious hard worker and a devoted father. He puts in long hours to assure financial stability. He feels it's his manly duty to provide the finer things in life. A big house, two cars, sports equipment, dance lessons, vacations, friends, family outings, televisions, computers, gadgets—lots of gadgets—and clothes, clothes that the kids will outgrow before the outfits wear out. James doesn't have spare time to ride his bike anymore. He drinks to unwind.

Alice is a delightful woman, a spirited mother and a supportive friend. She can do anything. She put her career as a graphic designer on the back burner to be a stay-at-home mom. She likes the role, but it often feels as if something is missing. She cooks healthy meals, packs lunches, manages a cozy home, and volunteers at the library. She taxis the kids to and from; in between she checks on her parents and her invalid mother-in-law. She entertains, attends aerobics and yoga, and arranges the family's social calendar. She is a master gardener, with roses climbing over the fence and fresh herbs growing on the windowsill. Alice is amazing and anxious.

Alice and James are good parenting and business partners, focused on their projects, skilled taskmasters. Who would guess that they go for weeks without making love? They ramble about to-do lists, but never talk about love or sex directly. They don't know how to begin a conversation about such a highly charged subject, so they squelch themselves and resort to innuendo. She notices him glancing at pretty girls and scolds. He notices her watching romantic comedies, but rather than asking directly what her interest might be, he is sarcastic about it. They swallow their no-sex secret and hope that sometime in the future, when they're less busy, they'll have the inclination to make love.

When asked, they agree that they love each other. But in private, alone, they wonder, Is it over? Did they fall out of love? They're sad. Very, very sad. When Alice lashes out James shakes his head and withdraws. He refuses to talk. She cries and feels rejected. They give up. He sleeps on the couch in the den until she urges him back to bed. They fall asleep, scared and helpless and losing hope. Alice and James feel lonely and they miss each other.

Is there hope? you wonder. Is it possible to regain the thrill of touching each other? Can Alice and James connect again?

Yes.

The answer is: Yes. Yes. Yes.

It is possible, but not as simple or quick or easy as we

might like it to be. There is no pill or magic wand. A vacation without the kids will not do the trick. Rekindling passion requires dedication, education, more questions, fewer answers. To reconnect they'll need to launch an inward journey. They'll need to look inside and dig deeply. They'll have to be very, very honest.

The great spiritual teachers from Buddha to Jesus, the brilliant psychoanalysts from Carl Jung to Erich Fromm, the philosophers and poets from Kabir to Simone de Beauvoir and Maya Angelou remind us that the seduction of the outer world is temporary, while the peace and joy found in the inner world is eternal. Unless we look inward, life loses luster. James and Alice are superstars in the outer world but their inner lives are sadly lacking. In accomplishing so much, in doing so much, in pleasing others, in securing their futures, running so fast, it's as if they've morphed from human beings into human doings. Like exquisitely designed robots, Alice and James appear successful—but inside they're suffering. They've lost their spark. Intent on building the life they thought they should build, they forgot to check in with what they needed. They forgot to listen to the wise little voice within.

What does looking inward have to do with day-to-day life, love, sex, and happiness? you might ask. Well, my dear sweet reader, the answer is: everything. If you don't know who you are or how you feel, if you're uncomfortable in your own skin, if you don't know what makes you tick and tingle, if you're afraid to communicate your urges

and longings, if success is the measure of your worth, if you're using sex to calm your nerves and hide disappointment, there is no lovemaking. You can fake connection for a short time, but if you're in a relationship for the long haul, you have to be authentic. If you want to make love, you have to unite with each other. To unite you have to be awake, aware, and fully alive. You have to slow down and take a deep breath. You have to be mature enough to know yourself and mature enough to respect your beloved.

LOVE LESSON

1. Consider this: A relationship is as unique as the two people who create it, but we can gain insight into our own relationship from hearing about others. Is there anything about Alice and James's relationship that reminds you of your own?

2. Be well. Let me say this in another way: Do not beat yourself up. Be gentle and kind. The kinder you are to yourself, the kinder you will be to your sweetheart.

3. Give credit. I am certain that you have done many things to be pleased about, and so has your partner. Acknowledge all your strengths. If you don't know what your strengths are, ask a friend to tell you.

4. List your personal priorities. Write down everything that matters to you. Don't edit. Read this over and put a star by your top 10 priorities. Priorities change, and yours will too. This is an exercise in reflecting on what matters to you. Ask your partner to do the same.

5. Each week, read a passage of poetry, philosophy, or a spiritual text. Try Kabir, Hafiz, or Mary Oliver.

SUSTAINING LOVE TAKES SUSTAINED EFFORT

If there was a silver lining to James losing his job in the economic downturn, it was this: he fell into a funk and had an identity crisis. For a man who wanted his father's approval and defined himself by his successes and how well he supported his family, it was a devastating blow to his superman image. It is not easy for such a man to find his center. In fear and despair he returned to riding his bike, the thing that brought solace as a child. Every morning, come rain or shine, he rode his bike 27 miles into the countryside and walked along the river. For the first time in years, James had the motivation to look at himself and the choices he'd been making. He began asking questions: Who am I? What matters? Where am I going? How do I want to live?

Thomas Merton wrote, "What can we gain by sailing to the moon if we are not able to cross the abyss that separates us from ourselves? This is the most important of all voyages of discovery, and without it, all the rest are not only useless, but disastrous." Or as Socrates put it, "The unexamined life is not worth living."

Silently riding his bike and walking by the river, James began to slow down enough to hear his own thoughts. This routine became his daily meditation. As he let go of who he thought he was and what he thought he should be, James turned away from reacting to his circumstances and toward reflecting on where he might focus in the next stage of his life.

The disconnection between James and Alice continued, however. James rode his bike, logged on to the computer, accompanied the kids on outings. Alice managed the household and kept the routine going. James withdrew and was tight-lipped about the insights he was gaining. He didn't intend to return to work in the same driven way and he didn't want to continue the lavish lifestyle they were leading. He wanted something different. He felt guilty speaking about his transformation. Alice walked on eggshells. Instinctively she knew the value of James unwinding, she sensed that a shift was coming, and she was worried about what that could mean.

At every crisis it is absolutely necessary to have friends to turn to. Alice turned to a women's group. The women commiserated and prayed, laughed and cried, shared secrets, worried and brainstormed. In the comfort of trusted friends Alice poured out her heart and discovered that what she was missing was James. With that realization, Alice took a step forward. One evening she slipped into the den, where James was on the computer, and instead of talking at him or flooding him with questions as she normally did, she walked quietly behind him and placed her hands on his shoulders. Instantly she felt his shoulders drop. He leaned back and let out a sigh. Not a word was spoken between them, but with that one gesture she felt relief too. Peaceful silence filled the room. There was no complaining or conversation. Two days later she reached out again. On the fourth day, as she rubbed his shoulders, James turned around and pulled Alice onto his lap. They kissed tenderly and that night made love for the first time in months. The following morning Alice told James she had arranged a sitter and asked if they could spend the day together. Within a month James and Alice were riding bikes together to the river. Without prodding, James began sharing and Alice began listening. They were communicating more than they had in years.

It boils down to this. Your day depends on you. The quality of your relationship depends on you. If you feel disconnected, so does your partner. If you ignore your partner, chances are, you are ignoring yourself too. If you blame your partner for what is wrong, you've probably been blaming yourself too. If you keep this pattern going, you will miss an opportunity to make things better. If you continue to approach your situation in the same way you always have, you'll drift further away from a possible solution and a deeper connection.

LOVE LESSON

1. Mend disconnection. A pattern of disconnection is a pattern that you both are creating and feeling. Are you missing someone?

2. Have a makeover. If you think your relationship could benefit from a makeover, start with yourself. If there is a quality missing in your relationship, find out if there is a similar quality missing in you and address that first.

3. Revamp your lifestyle. Are you and your sweetie on the same page? Are your lifestyle preferences similar? When was the last time you evaluated your lifestyle?

4. Exercise. Move your bodies. Keep your body, mind, and soul in top shape. Ride bikes. Sing. Dance. Remember, it is impossible to solve your problems while stubbornly remaining the same person who brought them on. The situation you are in was created together.

5. Remodel. The only relationship impasse that can't be solved is when one partner is unwilling to look deeper and participate in creating a solution.

ODD COUPLE, PERFECT MATCH

There are no perfect couples, but there might be a perfect match. Ella likes vegetables with every meal, including daily breakfasts of roasted broccoli with scrambled eggs and herbal tea. Henry's food preferences lean toward pancakes and black coffee for breakfast, meatloaf sandwiches, pizza, and anything barbecued. "That's just the way I am," Henry replies to Ella's requests not to stuff the grocery cart with snack foods, not to eat on the couch, not to eat before dinner, and to wipe the crumbs from his sweater.

If any couple illustrates the odd couple united in a perfect match, it's Henry and Ella. Together they're a bundle of contradictions. Henry's laid-back and distracted, sociable yet never on time. Ella's the opposite, highly organized and always on time. Her closet and desk are immaculate, while his desk is covered in papers and his car hosts banana peels and candy bar wrappers. Accommodating his sloppiness with her vigilance is quite a balancing act. They get on each other's nerves.

Ella shouted, "You could drive a saint insane" when she saw his dirty dishes piled in the sink. "How many times do I have to tell you put your dishes in the dishwasher?"

"You're a control freak," Henry accused. "The kitchen is the wife's job, the men in my family don't do dishes."

Ella threw herself on the bed and sobbed, wishing she

43

hadn't lashed out while Henry sat in the big chair, head in his hands, shaking. Chest pounding, he didn't like the way she ordered him around but he hated the way he spoke to her. They both felt horrible. But with apologies and makeup kisses, they entered a new phase of their relationship—discovering aspects of their own and each other's personalities that they hadn't expected.

We're all works in progress. No one is perfect—even the sweetest of sweethearts displays annoying habits. Perhaps you're finding out about your sweetheart's habits, as your sweetheart is finding out about yours? Ella and Henry are encountering feelings they've never expressed before and they try to work them through. And they do work some of their feelings through—although in the beginning they hardly know what that meant—and the bond between them grows deeper and they became more committed. Then deeper issues come up, and they work those through too. That's how relationships get built and that's how trust develops and that's how love grows. The disappointment and the anger and the hurt all get transformed in some way, and it's nothing less than miraculous.

Our sweetheart offers us the very things that we are not so good at, shows love in ways we never dreamed. Our sweetheart teaches us what we don't know, does things we can't do, comforts us when we can't comfort ourselves. By appreciating what he or she gives that we can't give ourselves we bring out the best in our sweetheart and in ourselves.

LOVE LESSON

1. Grow up. Although it might come as a surprise that normal grown-up adults need to be constantly growing and learning, that is exactly what is called for in a perfect match. The more willing you are to learn and grow, the more perfect your match will be.

2. Be a work in progress. A relationship is not a settling down, but rather a lively journey, a process of growth and movement. Neither of you is finished; both of you are works in progress.

3. Accept humanness. Accepting quirks and vulnerabilities in your beloved is the way to slowly make peace with your own. Accepting humanness is what makes the perfect match.

4. Allow differences. Differences of opinion are not a betrayal of the relationship but rather something to be expected, something that will further growth.

5. Develop. The qualities you need to become a loving partner are the same qualities you need to be a loving person. A relationship is the training ground to become the person you are meant to be.

COME TO GRIPS WITH DISCORD

Moving in with your sweetheart is like going to Paris. You see a colorful brochure of the City of Light with chic people riding bicycles, drinking wine in smoke-filled cafés, and smooching under the Eiffel Tower. You want to experience that, so you save your pennies, book a ticket, and after a grueling airplane trip you arrive. You're eager to stroll along the Seine and view the Mona Lisa but your partner has leftover motion sickness. All he wants to do is take a nap and study the visitor's guide. Strain erupts over where to eat your first dinner. Reality whittles away your fantasy. He is ready to go back to the hotel after broth and you want to linger over boeuf bourguignon.

Living together is a lot like looking at a travel brochure and planning a vacation. We have expectations and a vision of what our life together will be. It's wonderful to be in love. It's wonderful to be loved. Everything is delightful. You feel so exhilarated that you can't imagine things will ever be different. And yet things get different very quickly.

"When we are getting along it's great between us," Marsha says.

"Yup, but when we fight it gets ugly fast," Victor adds. Sweethearts clash whether they are traveling or staying home. If you don't deal with conflicts, they gather momentum until one day nothing can stop them and they thunder down on you like an avalanche.

What does learning to deal with conflict mean? One thing it means is understanding that a lovers' quarrel does not have to be the end of the world. Lovers can disagree and argue and get mad, and the love can still be there. Fighting can teach you some marvelous lessons. One of the most valuable things quarreling lovers get to experience is the sequel to raising their voices and hanging up the phone on each other. The next time they meet—still mad, in all probability—well, it's this way: she looks at him, he looks at her, and suddenly everything is all right again. That's a wonderful experience. And there's no way they could have had it without that lovers' quarrel. In fact, that's why a lot of people fight—because there's nothing like the thrill of making up. You can't experience making up without first having a quarrel. Closeness and intimacy sometimes seem to require quarreling. Sometimes it takes fighting and sticking up for yourself too. And there is nothing wrong with fighting as long as it results in growth and realization, in some insight and understanding, in something constructive.

LOVE LESSON

1. You. Will. Quarrel. Don't. Take. It. So. Seriously.

2. Take it as an opportunity to clarify expectations. A quarrel may be an indication of unspoken expectations. Think about your own expectations and ask about your sweetie's. "What are you expecting?" is a good question if asked sincerely and said tenderly.

3. Maintain a productive spin. Fighting occasionally is healthier than never fighting. It's how underlying issues get exposed. It's how old wounds are brought to the surface so they can heal. Without at least some openness to fighting, everything just festers. Say, "Let's figure this out together."

4. Respond positively to every comment—no matter how small—that moves you and your partner in the direction of clarifying and understanding.

5. Look for the constructive. What seed of understanding have you gained, what insightful tidbit? When things cool down, share your realizations.

ARTFUL ACTION

The potential that daily love inspires in us is miraculous. If we want to get good at any art—including the delicate art of caring for each other—we must practice daily. Practice. Practice. Practice. It is in negotiating work and family life, navigating dreams and daily reality, striving for balance between passions and tending the humdrum, that we practice and perform the full spectrum of artful loving action. The first principle of artful action is: Your sweetheart is not you. The second principle is: You can enjoy the differences.

Artful action is assuming the best even when your partner is less than what you expected. It's having an argument and letting go of that argument for the good of your relationship. It is looking into the face of your beloved and seeing what lies in the heart. Artful action means turning things around even if your spouse is not cooperating; not hurting your sweetheart just because you are hurting; taking a deep breath and counting to 100. Artful action is knowing when to speak up and when to be still. It's putting yourself in your sweetheart's shoes and empathizing. It's the determination to find the silver lining when things are bleak. Admitting you are wrong and apologizing and accepting your sweetheart's apology too. It's forgiving. Artful action is based on the principle that we cannot twist our partner to fit our own image. Artful action is the deep assurance that you alone have the capacity to make your day meaningful and joyful.

Ethan and Emma were embroiled in typical newlywed disagreements. You know those first rumblings that stir discontent, like buyer's remorse? Fueled by the shock that settles in after the excitement of being married wears off, Ethan and Emma were coming up against issues they hadn't noticed before—how to squeeze the toothpaste, whether or not the toilet lid should be left up or down, and if it's okay to drink straight out of a carton.

In the heat of yet another argument Emma burst into tears. "All we do is fight," she said.

Ethan pulled her close and said, "These fights are good for us. I'm becoming a better person because I have to figure out how to make it better for both of us. You're helping me do that."

In Chinese philosophy yin and yang are complementary opposites that make up a greater whole. Your sweetheart is in many ways the opposite of you. Experts theorize that our partner is a mirror to the hidden parts of our own personality. That could explain why an extrovert chooses an introvert, an optimist falls for a pessimist, an accountant chases a dancer, a neatnik marries a slob. To get along with your opposite you'll need to sharpen your skills and surrender to what love asks of you. "I want to behave well," Ethan told me. "My wife makes every day bearable. When I didn't get the job I wanted, I wasn't devastated, because I knew she believed in me." With artful action your commitment becomes a spiritual practice. A chance to uncover the wonder and awe within yourself and within the person you chose to be your teacher. Artful action does not mean sacrificing your essence but rather opening to another. Genuine love does not squelch the other, it lifts both lover and beloved closer to their wonderful selves.

LOVE LESSON

1. Memorize the artful actions principles:
   My sweetheart is not me.
   I can enjoy the differences.

2. Learn the language of love. The language of love is more poetry than mathematics, deeper than what appears on the surface. Love language stirs the soul and speaks to our longings.

3. Do nothing, and do it artfully. When you don't know what to do, don't do anything at all. But do nothing artfully. Say, "Honey, let's give ourselves the benefit of all doubt. Let's assume the best."

4. Make the artful choice. There is always an artful choice. If you don't like what is going on between the two of you, use an artful approach. Make love a self-transformation and your life will be enriched.

5. Develop skills. Infuse daily life with artful action. Ask yourself: How can I approach the day with an artful attitude?

MAKE ROOM FOR GROWING PAINS

Adult growing pains, in the form of a midlife crisis or existential crisis, can strike at any moment. The pain is often intense and confusing. Like children whose growing pains wake them in the middle of the night, adults suffering growing pains may toss and turn throughout the night, awake with a feeling of dread, and act out in uncharacteristic ways. Such hidden rumblings, like an earthquake under the surface, are signals of adult growth and development in the making. As 10- and 12-year-olds feel growing pains in their legs and muscles after a day of jumping and running, adults too suffer pangs with maturing.

The deep dilemmas of everyday love are subtle. They are more meaningful than snafus such as whose turn it is to cook dinner, more advanced than whether to purchase a car or a boat, more fragile than where to go for date night and when to make love, deeper than political leanings, religious affiliations, and familial ties. You may not recognize the subterranean quandaries, but be aware that they exist and need attention.

When his best buddy died in a motorcycle accident, Dillon could not sleep, even with pills. Then a major business deal fell through and his self-esteem plummeted. He went from thinking of himself as important to thinking of himself as a failure with no purpose. A big guy with a personality that fills the room, Dillon squelched distressing thoughts instead of examining them. Financially successful, he bought expensive cars, big dogs, and huge houses to allay uncomfortable feelings. Always looking for the next deal, he gambled on horses, rubbed shoulders with folks in high places, drank whiskey and had sex to relax. When those diversions no longer soothed the chords of discontent he was forced to look inside. His wife, Claire, who had been on an inner quest of her own for several years, wisely realized that Dillon's crisis was fueled by his feelings of inadequacy, shame, disillusionment, and insecurity. She let him know that, in her eyes, he was still amazing and desirable. With her understanding, 44-year-old Dillon began a painful self-examination.

It is not easy to look squarely at yourself or to stay calm while your partner has a meltdown. It is not easy to grow up. When we commit to another person we are often immature in our thinking about how love will play out. Morgan and Adam had been married for 19 years when they came to counseling, and it took them almost two years to admit the truth of their situation. They both were unhappy, withdrawn, sullen, unreliable, angry, and blaming each the other for their internal state. For years they'd been too busy achieving, too preoccupied with doing what was expected, pretending everything was fine. They didn't believe in divorce, so they ignored the small voice that pointed out that they no longer felt connected to themselves or each other. With their twins off to college,

Morgan and Adam could no longer ignore the distance between them.

Whether it's your identity crisis, your partner's existential crisis, or a midlife crisis that threatens the relationship, the inner truth must be acknowledged. To grow up and mature you have to let go of all those concepts you've been holding on to about what a relationship "should" be, about what true love means, about how a healthy marriage "ought to" function. Jade and Phil had been living together since they were 19, and by age 26 they were both in the middle of a quarter-life crisis. She wanted to go to Japan to teach English, he wanted to go to Hawaii to surf. Staying calm while sorting through their parents' expectations that they marry was a rite of passage for both.

Everybody, regardless of gender, race, marital status, age, economic standing, religious affiliation—pretty much every biological and lifestyle variation you can conceive of—has a crisis or two (or more!) during his or her lifetime. Why are we here? What is the purpose of life? Am I worthy? How am I supposed to live in this crazy world? Existential questions such as these are natural. Every relationship has bumps in the road. Every person has internal conflicts. Serenity and maturity come when we understand that no matter what is going on in our relationship, the quality of our well-being depends on only one factor, and that is how honest we are with ourselves. Our partner is not the overseer of our growth, our happiness, or our destiny. We are not the supervisor of our partner's growth, happiness, or destiny. We grow up by contemplating what it means to be authentic. We plug into joy and gratitude when we respond to our soul.

LOVE LESSON

1. Make room for growing pains. We have an inner world and an outer world—contemplate the inner. If your life or your relationship is not going as you would like, delve deeper. Is one of you in a quarter-life crisis, an identity crisis, midlife crisis, or existential crisis?

2. Get your ego out of the equation. In other words, don't take your partner's crisis as a personal affront to you. You did not cause this crisis, nor can you cure it. If your partner tries to make the crisis about you, stay calm and say kindly, "I'm sorry you are having a difficult time right now. I want to do whatever I can to help."

3. Reassure your partner that you do not blame the external world, your relationship, or your partner for your internal pain. Say this over and over: "You did not cause this. I don't blame you. I will figure it out. My pain is mine to work through."

4. If you have children, make your children's happiness your priority. Take extra steps to ensure that they are sheltered and happy, and they know that they are loved and have a strong family unit, even if one parent is in the midst of an identity struggle.

5. Take time apart. A couple can take time apart without parting ways entirely. Let your partner know that you are willing to work this through together while giving him or her the emotional space to do it.

REMEMBER BEING CHOSEN

Do you remember falling in love, choosing your partner, and being chosen? Four decades later, Millie and Wallace remember clearly choosing and being chosen. Millie met Wallace on a blind date arranged by her friend Betty. When Betty asked Millie to visit her at college, Millie jumped at the chance. Millie, then a 22-year-old divorcee with a three-year-old son, had not had a social life since divorcing her deadbeat, hard-drinking high school boyfriend two and a half years previously. Millie was unsure about being fixed up; in fact she was skeptical and suspicious. Even so, there must have been a smidgen of hope because she agreed to the date with the stipulation Betty tell Wallace Millie was a single mother.

The date was a success, and several months later Wallace asked Millie why she had insisted that he be told she was a single mother.

"I wanted you to know before it was too late," Millie said.

"The minute I saw you it was already too late," Wallace replied. And that's when Millie's heart chose him.

We fall in love for reasons known and unknown. That instantaneous moment of choosing is guided by forces beyond reason and logic. Proof perhaps that there are unseen forces working behind the scenes urging us toward love.

Antonia had been in a series of horrid relationships and had decided that she would never marry, never have a serious long-term partner. She didn't want one and wasn't looking for one. She preferred living alone. She had a great career as a dancer and was not interested in complications. Antonia met Joel while browsing in a record shop where he was working. She asked his help finding recordings, and Joel led her around the store, pointing out music that he thought she absolutely must have. He turned her on to new sounds, beautiful recordings of Handel and Purcell and Stravinsky. She bought so many records that she did not have enough money to pay the bill. Joel said she could return the next day to purchase them and asked if he could call her. He slipped her a piece of paper on which he had written her name and the appropriate number of spaces for a phone number. Antonia thought it was corny. So far, mind you, she had only looked in Joel's direction; she had never actually looked directly into his eyes. But after reading that slip of paper she looked into Joel's eyes. "Really, no kidding," she told me, "it was like a Hollywood B movie: trumpets went off, lights flashed, and my heart skipped a beat." She fell in love—in spite of her earlier decision not to—in an instant.

"A sudden relationship at this point, within days of my departure from LA for Boston, was definitely off the agenda," Joel says, describing that meeting. "So are sudden downpours, and gratuitous rainbows. But it happened."

LOVE LESSON

1. Remember falling in love. The story of your meeting and courtship is significant. Tell the story from the moment you laid eyes on each other and continue to the instant that you knew that the two of you were an item.

2. Tell your tale in its full romantic detail. All such meetings are romantic. Perhaps your story included chocolate and flowers, candlelight and diamonds; perhaps there was none of that. Perhaps your meeting was arranged. What makes your story romantic is the electricity flowing between you. Reminisce about the vibrant energy between you.

3. Describe the moment you first saw each other and heard each other's voice. What did you feel when you first touched? Where was your first kiss? What were you feeling, what did you say? Was it love at first sight or did love blossom slowly? How did your relationship progress? How and when did you officially become a couple? If you have pictures from those years, take them out and make an album. If you have teenagers, although they may not show it, they will especially like hearing your story.

4. Consider this question: Did you choose love or did love choose you? Chances are, it was not one or the other, it was both. Your choice was made for good reason. Rejoice in all the good that has come from it.

5. There are two versions of your meeting—yours and your sweetheart's. Listen to both versions. Hearing both is enlightening. Even if you are a couple who communicate more than others, you might hear something you didn't know or didn't remember.

CHAPTER III

SWEET SURRENDER

Joy and love are related.
They are not something you can force.
You cannot create joy
but you can create a space
for joy to enter.
You cannot create love
but you can create a space
for love to enter.
You cannot manage joy,
you cannot manage love.
Only when you surrender
can you experience
what love and joy
are all about.

NOT EASY BEING A SWEETHEART

You've probably experienced how your sweetheart can bring out the best in you and the worst in you? In the morning, sharing the paper, sipping coffee, making pancakes for the kiddies, looking forward to the evening out together—content and optimistic—all is right with the world. Your kids are smart and cute, your husband's smart and cute, and you're feeling on the smart and cute side yourself. In those smart and cute moments your heart swells up so big that you think it might burst.

Later it's a whole new scenario. The kids make sandwiches, spill ketchup on the floor, leave crumbs on the counter. Your husband decides to remodel the bathroom. You're glad to get the project started but secretly question his timing. Proud for showing restraint and not wanting to stir up trouble, you squelch your observations. But two hours before you're scheduled to go out he's still tearing down a wall and removing the sink.

"We have reservations across town," you say. "Aren't you going to get ready?"

He doesn't respond.

"Are you going to get ready?" you ask a little louder. Still, no answer. To get his attention, you call his name. Firmly.

"What?" he answers.

"Why do you always do this?"

"Do what?"

"Why do you squeeze everything in at the last minute?"

"I thought you wanted me to remodel the bathroom."

"Not when we have plans," you snap.

"What's your problem?" he snaps back. "There's plenty of time."

Next thing you know, you're crying and slamming the door. "Geez," you hear him mutter as he steps into the shower.

After all I do for you, you're thinking. Later he confesses what he was thinking: I can never do anything right.

Without even knowing there are triggers, triggers get triggered. Buttons get pushed. Feelings get bruised. You hate to admit it but you're hard on your sweetheart and hard on yourself. You know it's impossible to get it right every time, but you want to. You expect to do better, you fail, you beat yourself up, you try again. You're tired and cranky and when your sweetheart asks what's wrong, you know you should be happy that he noticed, but his tone sounds more like criticism than concern.

"Nothing," you snap.

"I was just asking," he snaps.

Suddenly you're embroiled in a snapping match.

You'd like to reach out, kiss and make up, but instead you walk on eggshells for a while. It's hard. It hurts. It's very confusing.

"I'm sorry," you say.

You both mean it. You promise not to act that way again. You love your sweetheart, yet life around the home doesn't always go in the direction intended.

It is not easy to be a person. It is not easy to be a sweetheart. A lover. A partner. A spouse. A friend. A parent. A child. A companion. A confidante. Much is expected, so many surprises. That smart, cute side we're so proud of is not the only side. It seems there are multiple sides—our public side, our private side, and the secret side only our sweetheart knows.

LOVE LESSON

1. Count to 100. Try this dance step. Step back. Step close. Reach out. Do it a hundred times.

2. Fess up. Okay, you've done it again. Snapped and showed another side. Admit it. Give some breathing space. Apologize. Clean up any messes.

3. Give your sweetheart a break. You snapped. Your sweetheart snapped. It happens. But it's not the end of the world. It's only a snapping match. Take a shower.

4. Say out loud, "It's not easy to be a sweetheart." "It's not easy to be a human being." Laugh and say to each other, "We've got a smart, cute side and our not so smart, cute side. We're both human." Now go out to dinner.

5. Rejoice. You might be the luckiest person on earth to have the sweetheart you've got. And your sweetheart is lucky to have you. Order dessert.

MAKE THE HIGHEST CHOICE

Marc, an architect by day, plays guitar, practices nightly, gets together with his group once or twice a week and performs whenever they book a gig, which is usually on the weekends. That's how he met Leigh. Marc singing. Leigh listening. Both swooning. When Marc spotted Leigh in the audience, his interest was piqued. She had an edgy beauty that appealed to his artistic side. He was accustomed to women hitting on him, but she was self-contained.

At intermission, he walked directly to her table. "I'd like to get to know you," he said.

"Join us?" she invited.

Two days later, Marc called her, and they've been together for a year. No guy had approached her so directly before, Leigh revealed to Marc. "I surprised myself," Marc confessed. "I've never been that obvious before." With those confessions the deal was sealed, their future destined.

It was romantic in the beginning, but since then they've been losing ground. Every time Marc plays a gig, Leigh is haunted with insecurities. Every time Leigh complains that Marc spends too much time away from her, he is perturbed by her jealousy. Girls hit on him, and she wants him to do something about the groupies. Marc says groupies come with the scene: "Just because they hit on me doesn't mean I act on it." Leigh wants more weekend time and is tired of watching him perform. She complains about this to her girlfriends and they all agree: If Marc really loved her, he would sing with a choir not with a band. So with their backing Leigh collected horror stories of rockers and groupies. She collected incriminating evidence for building a case against him.

We can probably empathize with both sides. We could probably build a case against each one. That's because there is not a right or wrong answer—even if we took a poll we couldn't come up with a clear-cut solution. Some would agree with Marc's perspective and others would support Leigh. And even if one side won the argument, what difference would it make? What good would it do? Would Marc give up music? Would Leigh drop her possessiveness? Wouldn't Marc be resentful? Would Leigh be satisfied?

When the heart is open, the mind steps in to warn us. Love is dangerous. We are vulnerable. We are scared. The mind conjures up all kinds of reasons to fortify our fears that the one we love will hurt us. Watch out. You can build a case against your lover to justify what you want and how you're behaving, but your heart will know the truth. You can point the finger, blame the one you love, but you will not feel good. Justified, maybe, but not good. Love is not only a feeling; it is a practice. It is not only a gift; it is a discipline.

LOVE LESSON

1. Do not be disgruntled. It's wonderful to have friends to talk things over with. Sometimes venting clears out the cobwebs so we can see how our own reactions are contributing to our predicament. What are you seeking when you talk to friends? Agreement, validation, advice, another perspective, support, honest feedback—or do you just need to vent and get things off your chest? Whatever your motives, be careful not to build a case against your sweetheart.

2. Do not build a case. You can build a case against anyone, but why would you want to build a case against your sweetheart? Have you been doing that? Or have you been trying to understand your sweetheart's point of view? A relationship will meet some of your needs, but it cannot meet all of them. A relationship will give you some of what you need or want, but it cannot give you all of it.

3. Watch out for imaginary fears. Possessiveness is poison to love and hardens the heart. Jealousy is fear, and that makes us do all kinds of petty things. Fear kills love.

4. Make high choices. The highest choice is often the hardest choice to make. Without pointing the finger, blaming, making the other wrong, and without incrimination, the heart wants to love even when it is hurt.

5. Let go. If your partner leaves, let go with love. If your partner stays, love. Love is always the highest response.

RESPOND DIFFERENTLY

When clients first come to counseling I explain that I offer both long-term and short-term counseling.

What's the difference? they ask.

Short-term counseling is: 1. You tell me what the problems are. 2. I listen to how you've been handling those problems. 3. I suggest ways that you might do things differently. 4. You go home and do things differently.

Long-term counseling is: 1. You tell me what the problems are. 2. I listen to how you've been handling those problems. 3. I suggest ways that you might do things differently. 4. You argue with me.

"You can choose either short-term or long-term. I don't mind," I tell them. "Just let me know which track you're on."

Clients laugh and I laugh. It's funny because we are all guilty of resisting what might be good for us. We all can get stuck in a "You're not the boss of me" stance from childhood. We resist even when what is suggested might be helpful. Have you ever done that?

Rose and Gabe hit bottom when their anorexic teenage daughter was hospitalized with a heart attack. The psychiatrist said that the family dynamics were contributing to her emotional problems. They'd heard it before, but until their daughter's heart attack they'd been stuck in an old pattern of resisting what to others appeared evident.

"Tell us what to do. We'll do anything," they told me after my explanation of short-term and long-term therapy.

"Anything?" I asked.

"If you want us to stand on the street corner naked, we'll do it."

Pain is a powerful motivator, I thought.

"Respond differently," I said.

"What do you mean?"

"If what you're doing isn't producing the results you desire, respond differently," I said.

Rose and Gabe loved their daughter, but until she had that heart attack they'd been unwilling to participate in family counseling. They'd been praying that she would change. We've all done that. Hoped that the other person would change so we wouldn't have to. We prefer that our partner, our children, our boss, our friends make all the adjustments. It's not until we hit a dead end and see the futility in postponing it that we surrender. By the way, Rose and Gabe switched back and forth between short-term and long-term counseling. Occasionally they'd object to a new way of responding, but I didn't mind. Taking steps forward and then backward is a perfectly acceptable way of growing.

"Love is a verb," I told them. Don't like what is going on, respond differently. Stumped and have no solution, respond differently. Overwhelmed, respond differently.

Lonely, respond differently. Worried, respond differently. Angry, respond differently. Afraid, respond differently. Concerned about yourself, your children, your sweetheart, your family, respond differently. Troubled about violence, hunger, poverty, cruelty, respond differently. Relationship out of whack, respond differently.

LOVE LESSON

1. Respond differently. You have the power to change your circumstances. There is always another response, always a small modification to make.

2. Invite cooperation. If you are always sucking it up, speak up boldly next time. Instead of saying, "I don't agree," try "Can we come to an agreement?" You might find an improved joint voice.

3. Seek guidance. You are not alone in figuring out what responses to try. There is good guidance available. Talking your situation over with a trusted friend or a trusted elder, will get the ball rolling.

4. Look inward. We have an inner life and an outer life. When we gain insight into our inner life, we unlock the energy to respond to our outer life.

5. Open hands. Do not cling to, hold on to, or fight to maintain the status quo. Welcome possibilities that emerge from creative exchanges. Instead of saying, "You figure this out," say, "We will figure this out."

ADMINISTER A DAILY DOSE

Steven did not take his diabetes diagnosis seriously. He did not follow the prescribed diet and consumed more sugar and carbohydrates than recommended. This bothered Melanie. She tried all angles to get him to take care of himself—sweet-talking, pleading, lecturing, reasoning, whining, nagging, threatening. When Melanie insisted, Steven resisted, and a tug-of-war ensued. Eventually she gave up and threw in the towel. It was probably the throwing in of the towel that was the turning point for both.

One evening Melanie cooked a stir-fry with an assortment of veggies and fish. She made enough for Steven even though he would probably refuse to eat any of it. As usual he looked in the wok, made a face, and asked if she expected him to eat that. Instead of her usual responses she said, "I was hoping you'd give it a try." He didn't. She made him macaroni and cheese and told him not to worry, she would eat the stir-fry leftovers for lunch.

The next night she made another healthy dinner. Steven turned up his nose at the veggies and refused even one bite. He ate a bowl of popcorn, some bacon and eggs, and ice cream directly from a carton. This became their dinner routine. Alice cooked healthy meals from the prescribed food list and Steven refused to eat anything green. It was not easy but she dropped lecturing and cajoling altogether.

Occasionally she'd suggest that he might try the sugar snap pea appetizer or the salmon salad. She remained persistent but not pushy, relentless but not harsh.

In the process of letting go of demands that Steven clean up his diet, Melanie learned a lesson in serenity. Seven and a half months after initiating the healthy cooking regimen and daily recitations of the Serenity Prayer—"God grant me the serenity to accept the things I cannot change; courage to change the things I can; and wisdom to know the difference"—she casually referred to roasted brussels sprouts as the new french fries. Steven popped one into his mouth and ended up eating a bowlful. There were no "I told you so"s or "What took you so long?"s, just a quiet satisfaction as Melanie watched Steven enjoying the flavors.

Melanie may never understand why Steven resisted eating veggies for so long, but what she does realize is that when she turned over the reins there was more peace, calm, ease, trust, and contentment between them. Plus, in her situation, patience felt better.

Patience nurtures love. Patience, the purest spiritual gift we offer, brings hope without despair, trust without demand, serenity without anguish, laughter without contempt.

LOVE LESSON

1. Reflect on patience. Name a person who has been patient with you. How did it feel to be with that person?

2. Take a step back. Is there a situation that might ease with a dose of patience? Could you benefit from putting patience into action?

3. Make patience a spiritual practice. One day each week, practice patience by noticing how things change slowly.

4. Accept. You can't change your partner. If you expect your partner to do things your way, you will be constantly disappointed.

5. Recite the Serenity Prayer: "God grant me the serenity to accept the things I cannot change; courage to change the things I can; and wisdom to know the difference."

GENERATE A JOINT PHILOSOPHY

All you need to do is fall in love—the particulars will work themselves out, right? Wrong! When it comes to matters of the heart and daily life, love is *not* all you need. Communication is not optional. When we sign up for a long-term relationship we enter into a contract, and whether we realize it or not, there are expectations. Generating a joint philosophy helps clarify unspoken assumptions and prevents these assumptions from growing into full-blown misunderstandings or resentments. A joint philosophy is a small paragraph or list of statements that you and your sweetheart write together to define the values, actions, and goals that you will put first. The point is not to write something that perfectly encompasses all the elements of your relationship, but something that will help you open up communicate about what matters most to the two of you, take charge of it, and keep focused on it.

If you are used to talking about your relationship, this will come naturally. If you aren't used to this type of conversation, it may feel awkward at first. Rose told Jason that she would like to write a mission statement and asked if he would be willing to do this with her. At first he was hesitant and said no. After she explained its purpose, he said he'd think about it. Slowly Jason got used to the idea. One night over dinner at their favorite Chinese restaurant, they wrote the first three sentences: "Our joint endeavor is to create a happy, meaningful life. We will do that by mutual respect and truthfulness. We will work hard, play hard, be silly, sexy, and comfort each other."

Even if you've been with your partner for many years, you can open the dialogue by asking questions such as: Is our relationship what you expected it to be? What do you like most about our relationship? What do you like least? Is there a way I could love you better? Similar questions are raised during annual job evaluations—why not address these topics with your sweetheart? Remember, these questions do not need to be answered immediately or resolved definitively; rather, they are intended to start an ongoing conversation about the ways the two of you interact and organize your life together.

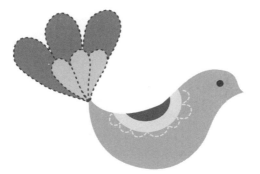

LOVE LESSON

1. Explain the purpose of your relationship. Say why a philosophy statement is important to you. Ask your partner to write one with you.

2. Be good-natured. If your partner says no or is tentative about starting, maybe it's because he never thought of doing such a thing. It usually takes people time to get comfortable with new ideas. Give him time to think about it and ask again in a few weeks.

3. Engage in an open dialogue about values, goals, dreams. This process is not about one person's opinions and desires winning out over another's. Work as a team. Identify three or four things you want to be the top priorities in your relationship. What things do you and your sweetheart want to share and work toward cultivating? Is it physical connection, spiritual practice, financial awareness, intellectual pursuits?

4. Write it down. Write a paragraph or a brief list that reminds both of you about your shared vision. Your language needn't be fancy or include everything you've discussed. If you identified physical connection as a top priority, what does that mean? That you will always kiss hello and goodbye? That you will have sex at least four times each week? That you will hold hands when you walk down the street? The more you talk specifics, the more likely you and your partner will end up on the same page. Put your philosophy statement someplace where you both will see it daily.

5. Take a walk, hold hands, kiss under the stars. Light a candle and make love for hours. Reevaluate your philosophy statement throughout the year. Like your relationship, your philosophy is a work in progress.

DESIGN IT

When they began hanging out together, Lydia made it clear to Jake that she did not want to marry. Furthermore, she wasn't sure if she ever wanted to live with anyone. "An ideal arrangement is separate residences," she told him. She cited her aunt and uncle, who'd been unhappily married for the two years they lived together, and happily married for 15 years after they moved apart. "They were headed for divorce until my aunt moved to her own place, which was within walking distance of my uncle," Lydia explained. She said the family was aghast at first, but over the years everyone settled down and stopped talking about it because her aunt and uncle were content with the arrangement.

Jake was enamored with Lydia—she was smart and sassy and beautiful—so he didn't give much thought to her position about separate residences, and besides, he wasn't looking for a serious relationship either. Still, when she talked about separate residences he sometimes played devil's advocate.

"How can we work differences through if one of us can slip out and go home?" he might ask. "Separate houses may be good for passion, but probably not for dividing up the chores."

Lydia was usually prepared with a well-researched

answer. "It's not as unusual as you might think," she told him. "It made Simone de Beauvoir and Jean-Paul Sartre intriguing, and that is good enough for me."

Lydia and Jake started out as casual acquaintances working out at the same gym, then progressed to coffee dates and conversation, slowly moving on to dating, agreeing to see each other exclusively, and eventually becoming a committed couple living apart. Oh, they do sleep over when both are in the mood. Jake, who fell into the arrangement, says it suits him fine. Every year, before Lydia renews her lease, they have an in-depth conversation about the arrangement. "We are keeping our future options open," they say. After six years their families have stopped worrying.

When it comes to matters of the heart no one is qualified to choose for you. Love has no borders, is not limited by race, sexual orientation, social status, or the opinions of others. A relationship is as unique as the two who create it and dwell in it. Love transcends all boundaries.

Daniel and Kyle, a committed gay couple, met in a support group for single parents with adopted special needs children. Since combining their families they've been on a love mission, raising funds for families like their own. Ian and Holly have their own love mission. When they divorced, they could not afford separate residences, so he moved upstairs while she stayed downstairs. They put fighting aside, devoted themselves to raising happy children, and through it all have finally become best friends. Henry is 14 years older than his wife, Katherine, and they both learned long ago not to base their relationship on what people think. When Katherine told her girlfriends that she was moving to the spare room because Henry snores too loudly, her girlfriends advised against it. "Sleeping in separate rooms will ruin your sex life," they told her. Katherine smiled. She knew from experience that a little separation makes love and lust grow fonder.

So what do these situations have to do with everyday love? Everything. It does not matter who you love or where you sleep; what matters is that you love.

LOVE LESSON

1. Imagine. Imagine love-filled days, love-filled relationships, and a love-filled life. Imagine that and make love your mission.

2. Take charge. You are in a relationship because you decided that this person would fit with you better than all other candidates. Let love reflect how special your beloved is.

3. Think about this. There are myriad ways to be together. Chances are you'll be more satisfied if you design a relationship that uniquely fits the two of you. Consciously or unconsciously, you are designing your relationship every moment. What do you want it to be?

4. Don't copy the Joneses. Who are these infamous Joneses everyone is trying to keep up with? And why would you want to run yourself ragged trying to emulate them? Instead of being concerned with what the neighbors are doing, adopt this policy: What others think of us is none of our business.

5. Rise above. Drop judgment of others. Love rather than judge. There is nothing wrong with loving everybody.

AIM FOR RECONCILIATION

Like most people, Loretta and Max came into their relationship with high hopes, excited that they'd found someone who was going to share their dreams. Then they had their first disagreement. It wasn't a quarrel yet, it was only a disagreement; they were still trying to compromise, be understanding, and overlook the small stuff. So they didn't express all their feelings or preferences. One or both of them sucked it up, but afterward a twinge of resentment remained.

Then, one day, they had their first real quarrel. It was nothing compared to the quarrels that were still on the horizon, but it was a quarrel. They got angry and said things they might not have said if they were thinking straight. Loretta and Max started expressing feelings they had never expressed before, feelings they never even knew they had. It came as quite a shock. They tried to work them through. At first, Loretta and Max hardly knew what "working feelings through" meant, but they kept at it—the bond between them got deeper and they became more committed. Then deeper issues came up, and once again, they worked them through. That's how relationships are built. That's how trust develops. The disappointment, misunderstandings, anger, and hurt all get transformed in some way and it's nothing less than miraculous. When you

clash you find out who you are really living with and who you really are. Strife can forge deep bonds. Disappointment is just about inevitable. Goes with the turf. I once asked a frequently married man whether he had fought with his wives. "Yes," he said with a smile, "I did, but not nearly as much as I should have." He reminded me of an important finding: the way a couple deals with conflicts is the single most important factor in reconciliation.

LOVE LESSON

1. Aim for reconciliation. If you're fighting on a regular basis, you are not understanding what your sweetheart is wanting to express. If that is the case, slow down. Say, "Help me understand." Or ask, "Would you be willing to take a moment to understand what I am trying to express?"

2. Extend bounce-back time. Word fights, like a slap in the face, are felt in the body. A heated argument with a sweetheart feels like a stab in the heart or a blow to the stomach, and that's why it takes a while to bounce back. Some of us get back to operating mode quickly, while others feel the effects longer and are slower to bounce back. Who bounces back quickly in your relationship?

3. Work through disappointment. Anger, criticism, hard feelings, resentments, chips on shoulders, sarcasm, poking fun, belittling, teasing, silent treatments—all add to disappointment. Working things through means hanging in there to understand and be understood. Once you understand what your sweetheart is trying to express, the door is open to come back together.

4. Say this: "Honey, what we both need is a good listening to."

5. Fix it. No need to hash things over and over. Fix, the best you can, whatever mistakes were made. Emphasize your common goals and your common desire to love.

CHAPTER IV

THE REALMS OF LOVE

How do you create a space for love and joy?
By wanting to.
By recognizing that you are capable of it.
By recognizing that
you are love at your core
that joy is your nature
and that anger and resentment
are the residue of wounds
that go far back in time.
The countless ways
that your sweetheart irritates you
are little sore spots
that were touched off almost accidentally.
He or she probably didn't intend to hurt you.

And if your lover did,
he or she must have had
something in their past
that hurt so badly
that they took it out on you.
Once you see all that,
you can, if you choose,
take off your armor
and opt for a beautiful
forgiving reconciliation
to take place.

"HONEY, I'M HOME"

"What's the proper protocol when coming home at the end of the day?" Lucy asks. Seems she and Connor have been bickering about—among other things—manners. If Lucy is home and Connor arrives later, should he find her and say hello or should she drop what she's doing to greet him? At the end of hectic days, Lucy and Connor barely notice each other. Lucy, who has been home with the kids all day pining for adult conversation, is hoping that Connor will sweep her up from the floor she's mopping. Connor, who has been in meetings all day designing advertising campaigns, walks through the front door hankering for silence. Unlike the lovers who run across the field and fall into each other's arms, Lucy and Connor are headed for a collision. She wants to visit. He wants silence for unwinding.

Although end-of-the-day reunions are not what motivates couples to seek counseling, homecomings can magnify tiny glitches. Taking off work hats and slipping into sweetheart mode requires an identity shift. Switching from daytime roles to family routines is a tricky transition.

Coming home is top of the list of Joel and Greta's favorite activities. Whoever gets home first puts out a plate of snacks and uncorks the wine. Whoever arrives home next heads for the kitchen. They hug, they kiss, and notice the look on their sweetie's face. "Having a bad day? Come tell me all about it." That was before the baby was born. Now they've added diapering, bathing, and cooing over how ultracute and smart baby is.

Some days, neither Jon nor Patricia is in the mood to say "Hi." And that's okay with them. Jon comes home and does his thing. Patricia is already home absorbed in her thing. After an hour or so of doing their own thing they're ready to be together.

Home is sanctuary, a safe haven where families unwind and relax with people they like and trust. If you care about your own happiness, take care of your sweetheart's happiness too, because happiness happens only in a happy climate. Saying "Honey, I'm home" with a harmonious vibrancy increases everyone's happiness. When body language matches words, when facial expressions tell the same story, happiness is contagious. Say it: "Honey, so happy to see you." Say it with words, smiles, squeezes, a twinkle in your eye, excitement in your voice. It doesn't matter who says it first, it matters that you show it. Your relationship is not a prison; it is not a job. Your relationship is a treat, a luxury, pure pleasure. When you reunite after being apart, give your sweetheart the respect, gratitude, and giddy joy that you would give to a great blessing that came into your life.

LOVE LESSON

1. Plan happy homecomings. What is your favorite home-coming reunion? On a scale of 1 to 10 (10 = the best), how would your rate the greetings you've been giving each other lately?

2. Remain in the right frame of mind to make the workday transitions. Remember, you chose this arrangement. No one forced you into sharing a zip code and a front door. Even if you're not feeling as chipper as you would like, act as if you are. Greet your one and only and act as if you're really, truly happy to be home.

3. Set the tone. What homecoming rituals fit your life-style? Does talking immediately seem natural? Do you need private transition time? Do you want to tackle the chores right away? Homecomings set the tone for the direction the evening will head.

4. Make your home a happy place. The happier you allow yourself to be, the happier your family becomes. Ask yourself, Am I doing everything within my power to aid in my partner's happiness and create a happy home atmosphere?

5. Have a safe landing. How do the two of you shake off the pressures of the day? How do you want to be greeted when you walk through the front door? Find ways to shake off the pressures of the day as soon as you can.

UNITE AS FAMILY

They move in unison. The alarm is set to go off at 5:45 a.m. but they are usually awake and moving by 5:00. Johanna sits on her side of the bed, slips into her worn red slippers, stretches her arms above her head, runs her hands through her hair, and pulls it into a ponytail. On the other side Caleb arches his back, reaches to silence the clock so it doesn't go off, turns on the light, jumps up, and meets Johanna at the end of the bed. They sense each other's mood. They greet each other with an affectionate squeeze, a teasing pat on the rear, and a look that conveys leftover annoyance from not enough sleep. Perfectly timed, their individual movements appear choreographed; half asleep yet flowing as a harmonious unit, they begin another rigorous task-oriented day. Johanna takes a quick shower as Caleb heads for the kitchen to start the coffee and let the dog out. He plops himself in front of the computer to check email and news. He lets the dog back in and pours a cup of food in the bowl.

Fifteen-year-old Abbey pops into the bathroom to borrow mascara as Johanna steps out of the shower and reminds 13-year-old Zac for the second time to get up. Zac groans, pulls the covers over his head, and rolls over. In the midst of another hectic weekday morning, information about work schedules, soccer practice, music lessons, and social calendars is exchanged in a flurry over a choice of hot oatmeal or leftover quiche, and they're off in separate directions. "Drive careful." "Have a good day." "Don't forget your homework." "Call me later." "Love ya." "Love ya back."

By 7:00 p.m. the family is home, and though a plethora of dangling details need attention, Johanna and Caleb are in agreement about what matters at the end of the day. The homework does not have to be perfect, the dishes can sit in the sink, unfinished projects will wait on the back burner. What is important is unwinding, decompressing, and breathing space to laugh and let loose, downtime to reflect and create. Tomorrow each will again put one foot in front of the other and do what is required, but tonight, under the same roof, they are chilling out and settling in. Johanna and Caleb intend to have family night. They plan to play a board game, eat ice cream, and experience the joy of being a family.

LOVE LESSON

1. Hold your intention. What is your love objective? In the realms of love, what do you want to achieve? What mood do you want to create? How do you want to spend each day, each evening, the weekend? What do you want family life to be?

2. Make your intentions known. Let your sweetheart, your children, and friends in on your love intentions. Ask about theirs.

3. Be your intentions. It is not who you say you are, but who you are. It is through your words, through your attitude, through your actions, through your responses, that others come to know who you are.

4. Hold positive intentions. Instead of dwelling on what is wrong, focus on all that is right. Instead of focusing on what you don't want, focus on what you do want. Instead of focusing on what needs to be done, focus on what you are doing.

5. Consider this intention: I intend to create a safe and loving home that encourages as nothing else does and nourishes as nothing else can. Organize the neighbors. Spread the word. Start a movement.

DO BE DO BE

The intention of coming home at the end of a busy day and letting the world go by as you settle into precious downtime with your family is great, but it is only an idea unless you have a plan to make it happen. Think about it. Busy-ness is the plague of modern family life. Kids are as swamped and overloaded as their parents, and their to-do lists are as crammed as their parents'. Homework infringes on playtime, after-school activities erode family dinners, chores and lessons gobble up daydreaming and imagination. Obligations infringe on romance and lovemaking, and with all that there is to accomplish parents are too drained for foreplay or pillow talk. When they find spare time, families are so addicted to activity and entertainment that they are unable to relax unless they are in front of one or more of their favorite digital devices. It seems as if families have more quality time with technology than they do with each other.

It boils down to this: if you want to spend satisfying time and have meaningful contact with beloveds, you have to make a commitment to balance "doing" with an equal amount of "being." Here's a simple technique that will bring awareness to where you're putting your energy. Get a large chalkboard or paint a wall with chalkboard paint. Draw a line down the middle. Label one side "To Do" and the other side "To Be." On the "To Do" side write all those typical things you need to do, such as these: pay light bill, pick up cleaning, schedule doctor's appointment, clean garage, plan dinner party, etc. On the "To Be" side list those rare and fine activities that bond a family together, those precious moments with no agenda, such as these: smile, sing, sit, stare, hang out. Put the chalkboard in a prominent place so that every family member can read it and add to it. The chalkboard becomes more than a list of schedules and obligations—it's the family message center, reminding everyone that hanging out is mandatory for good balance.

LOVE LESSON

1. Sing the "Do Be" song. Do Be, Do Be, Do Be Do. Repeat this phrase: I'm a human being, not a human doing.

2. Stop. Do not push yourself to be the perfect mom or perfect dad. Be Mom, that's enough. Stop. Be Dad, that's enough. Kids benefit when parents are relaxed enough to be present and not distracted. Catch your breath. Do less. Be more.

3. Encourage downtime, slow time, daydreaming. We all thrive with wide-open being time. Imagination develops, creative abilities and talents bloom.

4. Follow the kids. Kids are better at being than parents. Dogs are good at being too. Instead of going through the day at hurry-up speed, go through the day in kid or dog mode. Or as they say, "Follow your nose and see where it leads you."

5. Sit on the curb and watch the bugs go by. I often ask kids: "What's the most fun you've had with your parents lately?" One thoughtful 10-year-old boy carefully considered my question and responded: "Yesterday, my dad came home from work and didn't change his clothes right away. Dad said we could sit on the curb and watch the bugs go by."

TREAT LOVED ONES LOVINGLY

If you find yourself treating acquaintances and strangers better than your lover, you've got a problem. It seems obvious that we need to treat our loved ones lovingly, but do you know what? As a counselor, I've seen hundreds of couples and families, and one of the ugliest sights I've seen is sweethearts—who claim to be in love, claim to love their partners—treating each other badly. I have seen parents being downright insensitive to each other and their children. You have probably witnessed that too. It is upsetting, but with awareness we can stop it.

The first rule is to treat loved ones lovingly. Treat the people we love with care, compassion, tenderness, and kindness. When you are near your loved one, start watching. Are you treating your beloved with love? In small ways? Do you think of your loved one as a fine crystal goblet, a very fragile person, someone whose heart might break if handled roughly? Fine crystal is handled with gentleness. You don't just throw crystal into a dishpan full of dirty old dishes. Crystal is should be washed separately and dried softly. This is how we need to treat each other, as if we are all fine crystal.

Do you know what happens to a crystal glass if it's handled roughly, without awareness, without care? If you wash it in a hurry or put it away carelessly, you can nick the rim—perhaps only a tiny nick, maybe not big enough to see, but you can feel it when you run your finger across the rim. In the same way, little nicks happen when we handle our sweet ones without gentle care. You can't see them, they're not noticeable to the eye, but after a while, those nicks get larger and larger, and they weaken the fine crystal until one day it cracks. This can happen to love. There is never ever a reason to be mean. There is never justification for treating our sweet ones roughly. A little nick of unawareness can someday cause a major crack, and the fine crystal is shattered beyond repair.

Oh, and one more thing, just in case you have forgotten: you are fine crystal too. If your beloved is mean to you, that signifies a problem in your beloved. Don't take the meanness to be about you. Don't treat yourself roughly. There is never a reason to be spiteful, harsh, vindictive, or mean to anyone—including yourself.

LOVE LESSON

1. Be sweet. Use gentle words. It's good karma to be kind to each other. Speak with tender words, not condemning words. Make a list of inspiring thoughts and infuse your sentences with those expressions.

2. Look with gentle eyes. No critical looks allowed. A soft glance is reassuring and can mean so much to the person receiving it. Gentleness melts the boundaries of fear. A gentle look sends the message "You're safe with me."

3. Eliminate grudges. If you are holding old resentments tightly, you must let them go. Old resentments are big barriers to new love.

4. Repeat after me: There is never any reason to be mean or cold or distant or suspicious.

5. Pretend to be a love bunny. Fill the space around you with positive vibes. Imagine that you are a big soft love bunny and put out that energy. Watch out, because people everywhere are starving for kindness and they will plead to hang around you.

REJOICE! YOU'VE GOT KIDS

Once you've loved a child you are no longer the same person you were before that child came into your heart. Your heart expands when you become a parent. Everything you do you will do with that child in mind. Your relationship with the child's other parent shifts too. Daily routine is not what it used to be; plans, priorities, agendas alter, and so do budgets, vacations, activities, sleep patterns. You will not get a good night's sleep again until your offspring pack their bags and move out of the house. You will be prouder than you ever thought possible. You will carry their pictures and willingly show them to strangers. You will have a tendency to brag. You will not have as much money, either. You'll buy the kids shoes before you buy your own. You will not be the same well-dressed person you once were; you'll turn gray and have wrinkles, and still you'll worry about your kids. Once you have a child, parenting is your destiny.

Children are incredible; they stir up feelings you never discussed before and weren't aware of. Beth and Noah thought they were prepared—after all, how difficult could an adorable 8 pound, 4 ounce bundle be? Babies and children are attention grabbers and powerful creatures. They revise relationships and family dynamics. Beth fell instantly in love with baby but Noah felt pushed aside, annoyed, and he missed his wife's undivided attention. Beth was too tired and preoccupied to notice. It took months to figure out a satisfying balance.

The Smiths had a common complication too. Rick employed an authoritarian approach and as the kids got older he got sterner. Ruth was a softy and preferred giving the kids a voice in the matters that affected them. The kids quickly learned how to navigate between parents, but Rick and Ruth fought and went through challenging years before they agreed on a compatible parenting style. It all worked out, though, because by the time the kids had kids, Ruth and Rick had mellowed and their differences didn't matter much.

So yes, indeed, you've got kids. You bought a crib, brought baby home, and the world opened up in wonderful ways. Children teach us plenty. Who knew that cleaning up messes and wiping noses, catching bugs and building forts, chauffeuring, homework, loaning the car, sending them off to the prom and to college could be so enchanting? Your heart swells up so big that you think it might burst. You made room in your home for a baby and discovered that you have room in your heart for more. You love your partner, your children, more than you knew you were capable of. In fact you may discover that you have room in your heart for the whole wide world.

LOVE LESSON

1. Recite the parenting motto: "I am unprepared for parenting." Prepare for adjustments but realize that you can never be fully prepared.

2. Adjust timetables—there is BC (before children) and AC (after children). Think about this: daily life BC was both humdrum and exciting, but AC there is never a dull moment.

3. Watch for mood swings. While the kids are doing what kids do, you will go through parenting moods. Don't take parenting mood swings seriously. Use prenatal breathing exercises to keep from freaking out. The bottom line is: You chose to become a parent.

4. Don't overbook. When you try to be everywhere, you end up nowhere. When you try to do everything, you end up doing nothing. Do not overbook the kids or yourself.

5. Read my other books: *Wonderful Ways to Love a Child* and *Wonderful Ways to Love a Teen: Even When It Seems Impossible.* You will miss the kids when they move out. There will be plenty of downtime then.

YOU'VE GOT IN-LAWS

Nathan grew up in a family with five siblings. He likes noise, activity, and people hanging around. Lynne grew up an only child of a single mother. She likes activity and people too, but in small doses. Lynne gets overwhelmed with constant commotion; Nathan feels lost without it. They squabble about when to invite people over and how many people to invite. For him it's the more, the merrier; she lobbies for "less is more." He prefers an open-door policy so that family can drop in unannounced. Lynne tries to be a good sport but she's anxious when they come over unexpectedly. Lynne's and Nathan's family cultures were very different, but the realization of how that would shape them came as a surprise. If Nathan has a bad day, he calls one of his brothers. If Lynne has a bad day, she retreats with a cup of tea and a book.

In-laws are a lot like the weather. You plan a picnic and it rains. Griping about the weather doesn't affect the weather. Grumbling about the heat doesn't change the temperature. You plan a quiet weekend at home, and then your mother-in-law calls and insists you come for dinner on Saturday. You don't want to go, but your partner does. Moaning doesn't make the situation better. Complaining to your sweetheart about your mother-in-law will not change who she is, and chances are it might build a wedge

between you and your lover. So what can you do? What can you do if you can't stand having another dinner with your in-laws? Answer: You can be pleasant. You can look on the sunny side. You can be generous. You can say: "I sure am glad that your parents had you."

We all have memories that bond us to family. Parents, siblings, aunts, uncles, cousins, and grandparents make up our history. They know our past. Their influences formed us. If you complain about your in-laws it is likely that your sweetheart will take it personally and experience your comments as a put-down.

LOVE LESSON

1. Investigate the territory. Every family is a culture unto itself with traditions, beliefs, and mind-sets. Find out as much as you can about your sweetheart's family. The more you know, the less confused you'll feel. At a minimum you need to know what holidays are important to them and what foods they prefer.

2. Choose battles carefully. Do not put your sweetheart in the position of having to choose between his parents and you. Never put your sweetheart in the position of having to defend her family to you. Your partner can say what he or she wants about his or her family, but you stay out of the middle.

3. Keep it short. If you must complain about the in-laws, keep it short and do it in private. Tear your hair out and get it off your chest, and then find something positive to appreciate. If you don't agree with your partner's perspective on the situation, say, "I know you love your family and I admire that."

4. Use your company manners. Be respectful. Do not be confrontational. Make an effort to appease your in-laws. Show a sense of deference. Bend over backward to get along.

5. Tell your parents-in-law, "I love your daughter" or "Your son makes me so happy."

REALIZE YOU'VE GOT PARENTS

Many of the problems we encounter with our love relationships as adults are the result of things that happen in our families as we are growing up. To understand who you are, it helps to understand who your parents are. Your parents have been with you since your beginning. They helped shape you. Like it or not, they've influenced your mannerisms and your looks. Your morals and values were molded in part by what they did and what they said. Your attitudes toward your sweetheart were formed in part by how your parents treated each other. You may have consciously rejected the parts of them that you don't like, your differences with them may be huge, perhaps you sometimes feel like a stranger among them, but still they have a significant impact on who you are today.

Seth knows his parents love him, though they aren't touchy-feely and seldom say it. They show love by being interested in how he's doing and what he thinks. Seth married a woman from a family of huggers. Not only do they hug, they say "Love ya" at least a couple of times whenever they are together or talk on the phone. He appreciates that approach but he hasn't quite got the hang of it himself and isn't sure why it's necessary. His wife teases him about his reserve and says, "You're the spitting image of your father."

Parents can be frustrating. Even if you're among the lucky ones who enjoy spending time with yours, chances are you've also been upset over things they've said or done. This is part of growing up. Instead of seeing a parent as the all-powerful giant who does no wrong, you begin to encounter their shortcomings. Seeing parents as multidimensional frees us from being a child and helps us love them as they really are. In accepting their foibles we develop compassion and come to understand that they loved us the best they knew how. When a parent dies, it is a profound and moving experience. You feel exposed and vulnerable, as if the foundation has crumbled. Even if your parents loved you badly and weren't there for you, you may well feel the wound of not being loved. The death of a parent is the end of an era and leaves a gap in the continuity of our lives. If we had our parents' love, we grieve their departure; and if we never had it or didn't have enough, we grieve the empty space that never had a chance to be filled. When your parents die you may feel like an orphan, but you remain deeply connected. Love lasts forever.

LOVE LESSON

1. Make peace. Making peace with the past is the best way to ensure that the past doesn't intrude on the present. Understand yourself by understanding your parents' influences.

2. Evolve. Take the best of your parents. Improve on their qualities. Become better. That's evolution.

3. Act like a mature person. Be respectful. When differences arise with your parents, respond in your most grown-up manner. That's proof that you've let go of hurts and have forgiven. Proof that you are maturing.

4. Change the one person you can change: yourself. You can't change anyone else in your family. Let me repeat that: the only one in your family you can change is yourself.

5. Pick up the phone. Call your parents. Ask them how they are doing. Figure out what they might need, and do it for them. Surprise them—for no reason at all—by sending a card in the mail. Take them out to lunch and pick up the tab.

CHAPTER V

GOODWILL GESTURES

What do you really know about your sweetheart?
When was the last time you had a heart-to-heart talk?
Your sweetheart has interests and ideas,
preferences and dreams,
longings and disappointments;
do you know what those are?
Your sweetheart has physical side, a spiritual side,
an emotional side, and a rational side;
do you know how your partner
manifests each of these aspects
in his or her life?
If you want to cultivate lasting love,
you must view your sweetheart
as a dynamic and interesting creature
and engage him or her as such.

LET YOURSELF BE INFLUENCED

Couple #1. You might conclude that he is stubborn, selfish, set in his ways, controlling, and a difficult human being, and you may be right. Whatever she suggests, the first and last words out of his mouth are no, can't do that, don't want to, don't need to, why bother, that's stupid, not interested, among many other objections. No matter what ideas she presents to enliven their daily life, he is not interested, and that puts a damper on being together. She wants a dog; he says, "Dogs are too much trouble." She suggests a cat instead; he scolds, "You know I'm allergic to cats." She leaves her knitting on the dining room table; he reminds her to put it away. She wants a hamburger and fries for dinner; he expounds on the dangers of such choices. She's cold and turns up the heat; he tells her to put on a sweater and turns the heat down. No matter how encouraging or excited she is to step outside the routine, he doesn't see the need and poo-poos her suggestions.

Couple #2. Perhaps you would think a 29-year-old was old enough and experienced enough to see the warning signs when she agreed to move in with a 47-year-old bachelor, but they were in love and you know how easily potential problems can be overlooked when the daze of being in love is upon us. The fact that she should have known is not the point. The point is that he wouldn't let her paint the kitchen, wouldn't let her rearrange the furniture to make the house they shared a cozy home, and besides the fact that he earned five times what she did, he was stingy with his money. The final straw was his critique of her choice in music and turning it off every single time he walked into the room. She packed her stuff and moved out.

Couple #3. In this case it was the woman resisting her man. He liked anything that moved or had wheels—trains, trucks, vintage cars, new cars, racing cars, roller coasters, motorcycles, unicycles, bikes, wagons, dune buggies, buses. If it moved, he wanted to ride it. Sadly, she wasn't interested and sadly she was unwilling to explore where his interest might take her. When he invited her, she said, "No, you go." So for years he went alone. Eventually her refusals came between them and ruined their relationship.

The moral of these stories is this: rigidity is anti-fun, anti-play, anti-growth, anti-togetherness and anti-happiness. Rigidity will be the death of joy between you, killing all possibility of pleasure and expansion. If you want to expand and grow together, you must let yourself be influenced by what your partner offers.

LOVE LESSON

1. Let yourself be influenced. Your partner has much to teach, to show, to give, to offer. Let influence inspire you.

2. Take a personal inventory. Are you cutting off your nose to spite your face? Do you say no to every suggestion your sweetheart makes? Do you insist on only one way? If the answer is yes, watch out. You are at risk of becoming monotonous, boring, and dreary, and as my great-aunt Olga would say, "rather routine."

3. Break out of the box. Experiment with new ways of being. In other words, reinvent yourself.

4. Nudge gently. If your partner is a curmudgeon or a killjoy, don't join him or her in that endeavor. Nudge gently while maintaining your fascinating disposition.

5. Romp, fool around, make merry, be ridiculous. If you don't remember how, that means your days are not what they could be. Life is sweeter and lighter when you're floating carefree.

APOLOGIZE. MAKE AMENDS.

"I'm sorry I yelled," she said. "I don't know why I do that. I am trying not to snap, but I failed again." Then she reached out with the most sincere hug, the kind of hug that melts a heart. "You don't deserve that," she added, "You're always so gentle with me."

"Oh, honey," he said. "You give the cutest apologies and the most fabulous hugs. All is forgiven."

"I'm sorry that I don't always act from the spirit of my love for you," she said.

"Oh, honey," he said. "We're both learning."

If you have been in a sour mood and snapped at your family, if you have dumped frustrations on the ones you love, then you know that dumping doesn't feel good. We've all made boo-boos, jumped to conclusions, been edgy and cranky, pointed the finger, lost our temper, and been defensive. None of us are perfect. We say things we wish we hadn't. When that happens we must apologize. Sadly, some folks never apologize. They pretend nothing happened. They make excuses and dismiss it as "no big deal." They prefer to forget all about it.

If you are a lover you simply must confess and seek forgiveness: "I'm sorry." "I was wrong." "I ask forgiveness." An apology brings your lover back, puts your relationship into peace and harmony. An apology is not a designation of who is "right" or who is "wrong," but rather is the beginning of resolution. When we own up to our mistakes, we admit that we are imperfect. Fortunately, perfection is not a requirement for forgiveness.

LOVE LESSON

1. Apologize quickly. As soon as you recognize that you've made a little boo-boo, or a big one, apologize. It's really simple, yet really hard to do. When you make a mistake, apologize to everyone who was affected by your words and actions. Be happy for yourself that you're mature enough to admit when you've crossed the line.

2. Don't let yourself off the hook. When you have an angry outburst, don't let yourself get away with it. If you behaved badly in front of others—your partner, your children, the neighbors, the in-laws, your friends—the right and appropriate thing to do is to apologize to everyone affected by your outburst. For example: "I yelled at your mother and that was hurtful and embarrassing to her. It was wrong of me. I have apologized to her and now I'm apologizing to you."

3. No generic "I'm sorry" allowed. It is not enough to simply state, "I'm sorry." You must identify your misbehavior and include that recognition in your apology. For example: "I am sorry that I made fun of you when you asked me to take off my dirty boots." Generic apologizes are lazy. Step up and give a sincere one.

4. Drop defensiveness. Defensive postures obscure the issues, muddy the emotional water, and create more distance. You may not have meant what you said; you may have been teasing, but if the other person is hurt by your words or actions, an apology truly is the appropriate gesture. "I'm sorry that I teased you about your singing; that was insensitive of me."

5. Extend a goodwill gesture. To complete an apology means that you repair the damage. If you kicked a hole in the wall, fix it immediately. If you said a cross word or snapped, make amends by doing something that would please your sweetheart. Repairing the damage is an act of contrition, a goodwill gesture that shows your sincere intentions to change your behavior.

FORGIVE

Divine love may be perfect, but human love is not. Sweethearts hurt each other. It usually isn't intentional, it usually isn't even due to selfishness or carelessness. The hurts that lovers inflict are almost accidental, touching sore spots and the residues of deep wounds that go far back in time. Your sweetheart probably didn't intend to hurt you. And even if she did, there must have been something in her past that hurt her so badly that she needed to hurt others.

If you're a lover, you can expect to get hurt. Only people who are not lovers do not get hurt, but then they miss out on a lot too. If you're a lover, if you are committed to love, you are going to get hurt. It's as simple as that. And there's the other side too—not only will you get hurt, you will hurt your beloved as well. Hurt goes back and forth. Yes, if you're in it for the long haul you will have a go-around at both. You'll ask for forgiveness when you hurt your sweetheart and you'll forgive when your sweetheart hurts you.

Joella hurt her sweetheart, Matt, apologized to him, and wanted him to forgive her right away. But that is not the way forgiveness happens. Before things could return to the way they were before the hurt, Joella had to be patient and wait while Matt processed what happened.

A couple came to counseling a year after the husband had ended a four-month affair. He was baffled that his wife was not over it "by now." He'd done everything to make amends and didn't know what else to do. The wife knew that her husband was sorry and that he was doing his share of making amends, but still she couldn't move past it.

"Our joint money was spent on his affair and all I got was embarrassment and heartache," she explained.

"Honey, how can I make it up to you?" he asked again and again.

"I want to go on that cruise you promised."

"Great! Where shall we go?"

"I don't want to go with you," she answered. Turns out that the wife wanted an adventure that didn't include her husband—after all, his fling excluded her. So, after some negotiations, she took her best friend on a cruise that he willingly paid for. Two years later, after all the hurt and pain had been processed, she got her adventure and he was forgiven.

How many times do you forgive? Once? Twice? Or do you apply the three-strikes-and-you're-out rule? Do you forgive 70 times, or 70 times 70? That's up to you. I don't have a formula for it, but I do know that lovers forgive over and over. Holding a grudge is not forgiveness. Your relationship may endure, but love will be shallow. And if I had to make a choice, I would rather forgive than risk losing love, because I love love. I love because loving is its own reward.

LOVE LESSON

1. Allow time. Forgiveness takes it's own sweet time. Don't expect to move from hurt to forgiveness in a straight line. Forgiveness is a progression. (One might even argue that it's a progression that lasts a lifetime.) You progress; you regress. You take a step forward, then a half step back.

2. Wait. Don't expect to feel better immediately upon uttering or hearing the words "I forgive you." Pain ebbs and flows as you move through forgiveness.

3. Build on a forgiving attitude. Reflect on forgiveness as you give yourself time to figure out what the pain is all about. Then give yourself even more time for amends to be made.

4. Write. Whether you scribble furiously about pain in a journal, craft a letter to the person who hurt you, or you are the person asking for forgiveness, writing about the anguish helps you free up your thoughts and get clear on what needs to be learned and what needs to change.

5. Speak forgiveness. If you're the person who caused your sweetie's suffering, ask what you can do to make amends. On the other hand, if you are the one who was hurt, say, "I hurt. I forgive. I am moving on."

KISS AND MAKE UP

Art and Nicole have an unusual mating ritual. When they have a spat Art often gets so mad he slams the door of their eighth-floor condo and storms out. Nicole likes the tension, says that's how she knows he loves her. His storming out makes her feel affectionate! If she can grab hold of him before he gets in the elevator, she pulls him back into their condo and they make up—sometimes for hours. If she isn't quick enough, Art rides the elevator down to the garage, gets into the car, and stews for an hour or two before he comes home. Then he's glum for days. Why? He feels neglected because she didn't love him enough to get to the elevator in time to catch him. Seems that making up brings them close.

What is your resolution style? Do you quickly kiss and make up? After a squabble do you need time to recover your bearings before you reestablish your emotional footing? Are your resolutions dramatic? Is one of you a quick maker-upper and one of you slower?

The first five years of their relationship, Randy and Brent screamed and yelled until they both felt better or were too exhausted to continue. Then they'd apologize and promise never to say mean things again. After 16 years of fighting and making up that way, they got it out of their system. "We just wore out," Randy says, "Now we seldom fight. One of us usually says, 'Yes, dear,' or 'Sorry, dear,' and that's the end of that."

Whether you need minutes or hours to digest what happened, whether you need space to be alone before you talk about it, whether one of you is quick to make up and one of you is slower, the most important component of a forgiving reunion is your willingness to start over.

LOVE LESSON

1. Answer these questions: Is one of you a quick maker-upper and the other one a slow maker-upper? Does one need space to bounce back and make an emotional recovery? If you are quick and your partner is slow, be patient. Time alone to regroup is a component of the makeup process too.

2. Admit wrongdoing. Regardless of the size of your transgressions, have the courage to admit when you are wrong. Are there any transgressions, big or small, hanging over you? If so, take care of them appropriately.

3. Do your utmost to make up. When you understand the little or the big pain inflicted, when you are willing to discover something meaningful about what went haywire, then you are ready to make up and move on.

4. Forgive. Even if you don't want to, even if what was said and done seems unforgivable, look for all the smidgens that have potential for forgiveness and forgive those.

5. Kiss. Repeat: "I forgive you, you forgive me, we forgive each other." Kiss again. Forgive again, make up again, and again and again.

BEGIN AGAIN

Frank and Libby operate under a mutual motto: "Regardless of what happened yesterday we can begin again today." That motto was the boost that kept them united and pulling together after a flood ruined the new carpet, the freshly refinished floors, the new couch, the new paint job, and many sentimental possessions. After bawling, kvetching, moping, complaining, they agreed that whining wasn't moving them forward. "Enough," they said. "If we can't say at least one hopeful sentence it's best to wait until we can." Mutual condolences for what they'd lost, along with gratitude for what they still had, facilitated beginning again. If Libby fell into a funk, Frank reassured her, and she did the same when he was discouraged. "Let's not go there," they would say. "Let's focus on what needs to get done."

With no insurance to cover the damage, Libby and Frank faced a daunting task of figuring out what to do. Instead of withdrawing and retreating into gloom they joined in the expression of sadness. Some days, that meant crying while mopping up water, toiling past midnight hauling away debris. Other days, that meant taking a break, going for long walks, having a glass of wine. Regardless of the cloud of despair they fell under, they refused to let a worst-case scenario come between them.

Every setback, every misfortune, every catastrophe, every heartache, every unexpected turn of events has the potential to lead you toward emotional intimacy—or farther away from it. Troubles and tragedies bring you closer or tear you apart. Every action has consequences for your relationship. You can turn away and endure troubles on your own or you can reach out and bear sorrows together. It is your choice.

LOVE LESSON

1. Move toward. When trouble comes, reach out your arms and move toward each other.

2. Shift from "We can't do this" to "We are doing this." Shift from "There is nothing we can do" to "We can do something." Shift from "I can do it by myself" to "I will accept your help." Shift from "It's not my problem" to "It's our problem."

3. Be aware. Nothing you do lacks meaning. Everything you do and everything you say has the power, on the most subtle emotional level, to bring you closer or tear you apart.

4. Begin again. Cry, complain, mope, kvetch, but do not wallow. Stand by, ready to catch each other when one of you falls.

5. Provide a safe haven. When your sweetie is down in the dumps, be the source of comfort. When you are down, let your sweetie be a comfort to you. Count each small blessing out loud.

FALL IN LOVE AGAIN

"Is it possible to fall in love again?" they asked.

"With who?" I wanted to know.

"With her," he said sternly, pointing to his wife, who was sitting upright and rigid across the room.

"With him," she said, pointing simultaneously.

"If you want to," I answered.

"What do you mean?" they asked, almost in unison.

"If you're willing. If you're playful. Forgiving. Light-hearted. Then, yes, it is possible. To fall in love again."

"Could you explain?" she said, jotting notes in a pad on her lap.

"Falling in love again is not for the serious, the resentful, the pious, or the certain."

"What?" he said, seemingly more perturbed than interested.

I don't have scientific data to back my observations, but I recognize that loving feeling when I am around couples in the zone. Relationships go through stages: In love. Out of love. In love again. Somber, self-righteous, finicky folks do fall in love, but if they remain uptight they won't stay in love for long. Such folks prefer being right to being in love. They keep score on who said what. They correct each other on insignificant details and have an "I told you so" attitude. They're more like debate partners than lovers.

"Do you know any couple who have fallen in love again?" they wanted to know. "And how did they do it?"

"They were playful," I answered. "They stopped taking themselves seriously. They figured out that it is more important to enjoy each other than push or strive for perfection. They stopped blaming each other and let go of the need to be right."

Take Hank and Ellen, for example. When Hank recounts road trips that he and Ellen have taken together he often exaggerates the details to make his story sparkle. At one time this irritated Ellen so much that she would interrupt him in the middle of a sentence. "That's not what happened," she would argue. Her need to straighten out the facts was stronger than her desire to enjoy his version of their trip. Ellen remembers the exact evening when she recognized how abrupt and controlling she appeared. Hank was telling a story in his usual effusive style when she interrupted to correct him. Immediately the three couples sitting around the table fell silent. They seemed bewildered by her comment and the laughter stopped. After an uncomfortable silence a friend leaned over and whispered, "It's okay, we don't take his story seriously." What an enlightening moment for Ellen. That was her problem: she took everything seriously. What attracted her to Hank in the first place was his lighthearted, enthusiastic approach, and in that instant she understood that she'd been squelching the very thing she loved. So Ellen made a pledge to take a step back, to hold her tongue, to pause and lighten up. Once she stopped arguing and pointing out the facts, affection came easy. They became sweeter, softer, more laid-back. "Your versions of the story are more romantic than mine," she's tells him now.

People in love don't take themselves so seriously. They can be serious when the situation calls for it, but their capacity for play is unlimited. Lovers like being in love, so rather than fighting over who is right and who is wrong, they are relaxed about it. "You might be right, honey," they say. "It's okay, honey, I like trying it your way." "No problem, baby." These are not mere phrases but an esprit de corps that they live by. They would rather melt together than freeze each other out.

LOVE LESSON

1. Take a lighthearted approach. Don't fall into the habit of taking each other so seriously. The days whiz by so quickly, if you're serious you'll miss the excitement of being together.

2. Whisper sweet nothings. When was the last time you whispered something sweet in your honey's ear? If you can't remember, it's been too long.

3. Call each other love names. If you don't have a special love name for each other, you're living on the edge of a danger zone. Turn this around quickly by coming up with several love names that fit your sweetie's personality and occasion. You'll need special love names for private moments and for public moments when you want everyone to know how much you adore each other; you'll need one for easing the tension and making amends and another one for enticing wild abandon.

4. Drop niggling. Put aside arguing for one day. Do not quibble over small stuff. After you've mastered a day, try two. In place of quibbling, pause, hold your tongue, and look for something to be amused about.

5. Behave like a lover. If you feel the need to fight, immediately head for the gym. "Bye, baby doll, gotta work out my tensions."

MAKE REASONABLE REQUESTS

"If Derek loved me," Anna says, "he would know by now what I need. I shouldn't have to ask him." Many people believe that the most romantic relationships are those in which two people can essentially read each other's minds and know what the other person needs without having to communicate. If you loved me, you would know what I want and need and do those things without my asking. Right? Wrong!

I doubt that those relationships exist, but even if they did, they don't sound like the most romantic. To me it seems much more romantic to melt away your boundaries by becoming vulnerable and articulating both your secret longings and your basic needs. And when your partner chooses to rise to the occasion and give you the very things you have asked for—oh my!—that's reason to swoon.

Your partner will never be able to read your mind, but the more you are able to communicate and make reasonable requests of your partner, the more equipped he or she will be with the tools to give you what you need. So how do you make your needs known? By communicating in short, reasonable requests. By turning declarations into questions. If you make broad declarative criticisms such as "You never clean the bathroom" or "You never go to the gym with me," or "You never compliment me" or "You don't appreciate me," you're putting up barriers to good communication. Instead of haphazardly reeling off complaints, pause a moment and reframe them more clearly. "Will you do the laundry?" is a fine request if what you mean is "Will do the laundry this time?" But if what you really mean is, "Will you be more aware of when the laundry is piling up, and when you see that it is will you drop in a load?" it's more productive to say so clearly.

If you want your sweetheart to honor your requests, it is essential that you honor your sweetie's reasonable requests too. You will let each other down from time to time by forgetting a request, not taking a request seriously, or simply flat-out ignoring a request, but don't freak out. Take the letdown in stride and say with a smile, "You said you'd do the laundry, but you didn't. What is going on?" or "Can you explain to me what happened?" Give the benefit of the doubt. If your partner continues to disregard your requests, it may be time to seek the help of a counselor or to reexamine your relationship. It's not satisfying or fun to be with somebody who is not willing to meet at least some of your needs.

The more cheerful and playful you can be while making requests, the more likely it is that your sweetheart will cooperate. If you make demands like a military commander, the chances of your sweetheart following through are slim to none. Make your requests friendly. Say each one with a smile and a smooch. This is love and romance, after all.

LOVE LESSON

1. Save complaints for the complaint department. A complaint is not a request. "You never want to go to the movies" is a complaint. "Honey, would you be willing to go to a movie tonight?" is a request. This is a complaint: "You never listen to anything I say." This is a request: "Would you be willing to listen without interrupting?"

2. Decide what is reasonable. Sometimes, in the heat of a relationship struggle, it can be hard to know if our requests actually are reasonable or if we are being overly demanding and expect too much of our partners. If you aren't sure, get the opinion of your friends, of your partner's friends, and of a neutral third party. Gathering input can be helpful in deciding what is reasonable and what is not.

3. Compile a list. What are three reasonable requests that you would like to make of your partner? Ask your partner to make three requests of you. Set aside 30 minutes to go over your lists together.

4. Allow time to act. Once you've made your request, drop it and let your partner act on his own timing. If you continually remind your sweetie of your request, you are a nag. A nag is not reasonable. A nag is annoying.

5. Say thank you. When your partner meets your request, acknowledge her action with sincere appreciation and a big hug and kiss.

CHAPTER VI

SIMPLE CONNECTIONS

Love and freedom
are essential needs
of the soul.
Freedom
to choose,
to respond,
to grow,
to make mistakes.
Give your sweetheart
the gifts of freedom
and love comes rushing toward you
and takes you to new heights.

LET FREEDOM RING

"Don't look in my purse," Annie tells Justin.

Justin knows what she is talking about and winks at her. "Stay out of my wallet," he teases.

"Stay out of my purse and out of my wallet" has been an inside joke between them for over 12 years. "We may be married, but we are still individuals with private thoughts, separate belongings, and personal freedoms," Annie explains.

"It took us a while to understand that love and freedom are related," Justin adds.

There's a strange phenomenon that happens between lovers. It seems as if most people, once they've found their lover, try to hold on so tightly that neither has room to breathe. Well, this simply doesn't work! Strict control is counterproductive to love. Oh, I don't mean that we grab our loved ones by the neck and proceed to strangle them to death—no, we do it in much more subtle ways. We say, "When will you be home?" and when our sweetheart is a half hour late, what do we do? We rant and rave and scream and yell and throw a fit and accuse them of all kinds of things as though we owned them. And if our lover wants to have lunch with an old romance from years ago, we stomp our feet and pout—we threaten, and we accuse, and the love slowly, slowly fades.

Freedom is very important in love.

Now, I am not suggesting that you take a backseat and become passive while your mate has an affair. I am suggesting that you let your sweetheart be free. If you allow your loved one to be free, he or she will come back to you. I guess the real reason we object to our loved ones being free is because we're afraid—afraid that sooner or later they'll leave us. And the quickest way to ensure that they will indeed leave us is to insist that they always and forever relate only with us.

LOVE LESSON

1. Watch out for possessive tendencies. We do not possess anyone. Work as hard for freedom as you work for love. Allow freedom to choose, to respond, to grow, to make mistakes.

2. Maintain the right attitude. Freedom is the gift of love. No other gift is as important.

3. Make your relationship come alive. Freedom to be who you are and who you are meant to be infuses a relationship with liveliness. When you are alive and excited about the possibilities, you're very attractive.

4. Leave, if you must. If you find that you cannot grant your partner freedom because he or she is not trustworthy, it is better to part. You don't want to be a jailer; you want to be free too.

5. Respect the natural rhythm. You come together and you go apart, you come together and you go apart, you come together...

STAY SANE

"I love my wife, but I am not in love with her anymore," Charlie said, staring at the floor, unable to look directly at Mary. He didn't expect counseling to fix the situation, he told me, but he was willing to give it a couple of sessions.

"Not in love with you anymore" is a dagger to the heart of any partner who hears it. That statement marks the beginning of a potentially high-stakes blame game. It is the first falling domino that launches a string of crying jags, irrational rages, threats, slamming doors, comings and goings, hiring lawyers, separating assets, dividing up friends, establishing visitation rights—all ending in divorce and hatred.

Or it can be a crossroads, a defining moment that shows the stuff you're made of.

Mary looked as if she was having open-heart surgery without anesthesia when Charlie delivered the line. I love you, but. But. I am not. In love. With you. Stunned, she sat in silence. Charlie had told her three weeks prior to their first appointment that he had only married her because his parents thought she was the perfect match. Hearing his explanation in front of a stranger she'd only known for 20 minutes must have been humiliating.

There are many defining moments in daily life. Partnerships go through phases, people fall into slumps, change course, say and do all kinds of hurtful things. But the bottom line is that no one, not even your sweetheart, can coax you into misery for long without you signing up. We alone are responsible for our own responses and our own happiness. We have choices. We can react like fire-crackers, go mad and make a big scene. We can play the victim and spout injustices. We can convince ourselves that the cruel hand of fate has dealt us a losing hand. Relationships are not fair. Your partner can change her mind, walk out, fall for someone else, say cruel things, and inflict excruciating pain. We may wake up one morning to discover that we are no longer in agreement with the man we are sleeping next to. They've changed, or we've changed. Still, we do have choices: we remain in charge of our own responses. We can search for the center of clarity. Respond with dignity. Discover a glimmer of truth and hold on to the hope that keeps us sane.

That is what Mary chose. When Charlie said, "I am not in love with you anymore" Mary chose to stay sane. She let out a deep sigh and asked, "What are your plans?"

No matter how many times I have heard partners tell each other "I am not in love with you anymore," it takes me a while to absorb the aftershocks. When I hear someone say, "I'm not in love anymore" or "I don't know if I ever loved you," I understand that they are in so much pain that they must do something drastic. My heart went out to Mary and Charlie—both good people, sincere and hard-working, with dedicated parents. Married in their early twenties and now in their late forties, they had all the trappings of a satisfied life. With twin sons entering college, they were approaching the independence and freedom they'd worked so hard to attain. Except that Charlie no longer wanted those things with Mary.

"I love and respect you, Mary, but I am not in love with you anymore," Charlie replied to every question Mary asked him.

"What would you like to get from counseling?" I asked.

Mary looked to Charlie and he answered, "I'd like for us to be friends."

"I'll always be your friend, Charlie," Mary replied.

That's when I knew Mary had chosen the path of dignity and sanity. I have seen people employ all kinds of strategies to force a partner to stay, but I've never seen those tactics lead to greater love or understanding. Coercing someone who doesn't want to stay to be with you is detrimental to your own well-being. Even if you succeed, you are left saddled with doubt and longing, and before you know it you're both tangled in resentment.

Before Mary, in all my years of counseling I had never heard anyone say, "I'll always be your friend" in response to "I'm not in love with you anymore and don't know if I ever was." Most freak out—they cry, fume, beg, and lob accusations. Mary must have known that freaking out or threatening Charlie was self-defeating, because not only did she circumvent a freak-out, she rose above anger, hurt, and disappointment. "I'll always be your friend," she said again and again.

Charlie did not return to counseling with me, but Mary did. I met with her off and on for 10 months. Even though she was sad and at times disoriented, she never lost her way. "We were married so young," she said. She couldn't blame him. She did what she felt in her heart was right. The day Charlie moved out of the house, she kissed him passionately goodbye and said, "You always were a good kisser." Then she took the boys hiking for the weekend. During the next months she took up sculpture, which she'd dabbled in during college. She entertained old friends and made new ones. She stayed steady. Whenever she saw Charlie, she asked how he was doing. She cried, she read, she went on yoga retreats, and accepted a part-time job. On a piece of paper she wrote the deadline she had set for herself to decide the next step. If Charlie didn't come home by the end of one year, she would move on.

Eight months after Charlie moved out, Charlie moved back in. Mary welcomed him home with the one condition: that they create an improved version of their connection. He agreed to do that with her. She told me, "He did what he needed to do for reasons I may never understand. I did what I needed to do for reasons others may never understand."

I am not saying that Mary's approach is suitable for every situation. I am proposing that each of us is the author of our personal story. With every heartbreak and every major loss, we do have a choice. We can let the pain define and destroy our self-worth, or we can choose to stay sane and be victorious.

LOVE LESSON

1. Stay sane. It is a noble enterprise to maintain your own sanity even as the world around you crumbles. When life as you once knew it is crashing down, keep your eye on the prize. The prize is yourself.

2. Be the rock. You are your rock. Say this out loud: "I will be okay." "I am lovable." "Good things are coming." Say this over and over even if you don't believe it right away.

3. Take it hour by hour. Take care of yourself in the simplest of ways. Go slow. Do not rush. Make one tiny decision at a time. Get all the help and advice you need; take what fits and throw the rest away. Do what is in your own best interest.

4. Eliminate coercion. Coercing may achieve desired outcomes in business deals and politics, but coercion has no place in love. Love is another dimension.

5. Define your bottom line. What can you forgive, what changes do you need, how much time can you give?

SMALL CHANGES, SWEET RESULTS

I often hear sentiments such as "Can't teach an old dog new tricks," and I say, "Maybe." But I think it depends on what's in it for the dog to learn a new trick and the patience and expertise of the trainer. Sometimes it is the smallest change that produces the biggest results.

Marna, an artist and owner of an art gallery, and her perfectionist orthopedic surgeon boyfriend, Dr. Sam, have been together for almost six years. Except for one glitch, which they quibble over every other day, they're an adorable, compatible couple. Dr. Sam's perfectionism is an asset in the operating room, but when his fastidiousness spills into personal life it can be super annoying. Marna's go-getting attitude propelled her art and gallery to success, but her feisty tendency fuels their disagreements. When Sam points out flaws—"Your hair looks frizzy tonight" or "Your blouse needs ironing" or "That lipstick clashes with your scarf"—Marna leaps to defend and confront. The last time Sam brushed lint from her coat, she went bananas and called me to make an appointment.

"I don't know how to get him to stop critiquing me," she fumed. "I don't mind his business recommendations, but his continual comments on my hair and clothes are too much."

Marna's feelings and her reasoning were valid, and I am

sure she could gather a band of ardent supporters to insist that Sam's critical remarks were out of line, but I suggested that blasting him might not be the best solution. Even if she could grind him into submission, I don't advocate butting heads as the best approach for lovers. Badgering a sweetheart into altering their opinions is exhausting and counterproductive to romance and coupledom. Perhaps it would serve Marna's purposes better if she could make one tiny change in her reaction. I suggested that if she could respond differently to Sam's assessments, she might make headway. Responding differently is the magic that removes the punch from a fight.

She did it. The very next evening, instead of objecting, crying, arguing, getting furious, having a meltdown, pouting, freaking out, calling him a perfectionist twit, she reached over and touched him gently. "You have such a good eye for detail," she said. "I appreciate that you want to take such care of me."

Guess what? He smiled. He kissed her. She kissed him back. Slowly small changes in Marna's responses to Dr. Sam's critiquing did the trick. Slowly he caught on that being on top of the action in the operating room is good, but controlling your sweetheart's every move isn't.

Combining individual strengths appropriately doubles the power in a partnership. Sam's propensity for the fine points combined with Marna's spontaneity is an unstoppable combination for success and happiness. Instead of wasting energy quarreling and defending, it's more efficient to appreciate the differences and work in unison. By changing their knee-jerk reactions they could incorporate all their skill sets; they could stay on track, be organized, and have fun reaching their goals. Small changes make sweet results.

LOVE LESSON

1. Change your language. Use different words. That's right: replace fighting words with loving words. "Honey, would you consider doing it this way?" is better than "Why do you always do that?" "Take your time to think it over" is better than "We have to decide right now." "Maybe" is better than "No way." "Yes, dear" is better than "Who do you think you're kidding?"

2. Change locations. Talk about hot subjects away from home. Designate your home as the safe place, a sanctuary free of hostilities. When one of you is heated, take a time-out. Continue the discussion in another location over chocolate and tea.

3. Change your body language. Keep the tone of your voice calm. Turn the volume down. Do not sigh. Do not roll your eyes. Uncross your arms and legs. Drop your shoulders. Soften your eyes. Relax your jaw. Look directly at your partner. Show interest and look friendly.

4. Change the mood. If the mood is agitated and rowdy, speak softly. Don't match an angry tone with an angry tone. Better to keep quiet. If what you're thinking or watching or listening to is revving up the atmosphere, soften the mood with music and candlelight.

5. Change your spirit. You can change your heart in an instant. If your heart is closed, open it. Run toward whatever keeps your heart open. An open heart is a healthy condition.

TRIUMPH OVER WORRY

We commit to a sweetheart and assume that in their arms we will feel safe and secure from then on. In many ways we do feel safer, but in other ways we are afraid of all the responsibilities and decisions we face as grown-ups. If you think that you have to solve all the problems on your own, of course you will be afraid! Of course you will feel inadequate. If you think you have to do everything—pay the bills, raise the kids, stay fashionable, stay fit, figure out what to invest in, do all the things your doctor, your dentist, and your pediatrician tell you that you ought to do, cope with this and that, try to keep up—well, don't you sometimes feel overwhelmed with it all?

Fear and worry prevent us from being content and happy. We feel on edge and can't calm down. We feel anxious. Janey fears losing the people she loves, and that unacknowledged obstacle keeps her from being vulnerable to her husband, close to her sister, and relaxed with her friends. Scott worries about not being able to support his family in the style he feels they deserve, and that apprehension keeps him away from home and working long hours. Unfortunately Janey and Scott suffer in silence. He feels trapped, she feels distant, and they don't talk about it. Suffering in silence pushes your partner away. By keeping troubles secret, you close your sweetheart out and a disconnection grows. Fears build up until a crack in your relationships appears.

It is easy to love when we're blissfully happy and everything is running smoothly, but to stay connected when worries pile up, tragedies come, and crisis looms is work, day-to-day work. Remember the commitment: in sickness and health, in good times and tough times, in uncertainty and in joy? Let your worry mantra be this: We have worries, but we will not worry about our worries—we will overcome them.

LOVE LESSON

1. Reel your mind in. Keep it close to home. Don't let your mind run away with you.

2. Try the worry game solution. With your partner, cut sheets of paper into long strips. Write one worry on each strip. Doesn't matter how big or small your worries are; just write them down. Getting your worries off your chest and onto paper strips and discussing them with your partner is the first step in breaking the worry-alone cycle.

3. Create two piles: one pile for Yes and one pile for No. Read one worry out loud. Ask your partner, "Is there anything we can do about this worry today?" If the answer is yes, place that worry strip in the Yes pile. If the answer is no, put that worry strip in the No pile. Continue until each worry is placed in the appropriate pile.

4. Throw the No pile in the trash. That's right. Since there's nothing you can do about your nos today, get them out of the way and out of your mind.

5. Shift your focus to the Yes pile. Divide the Yes pile between you. Put your worries in order based on which one you will handle first, second, and third. Decide what action to take and do it immediately. After you have taken the action, move on to the next worry. Keep taking action until you have reached the end of your worry strips.

SAY NO TENDERLY

Leila moved in for a full-body cuddle, wrapped her bare legs around his, and snuggled up against his warm back. Neil liked it, for sure, but on that particular night he was really, really tired, "Oh, honey," he said, "that's such a good idea. You feel so soft and smell so good that I would really like to, but I am soooo sleepy. Would you mind if we held off until the morning?"

Leila laughed out loud. She didn't feel rejected and wasn't offended; it was such a tender no. In fact one of the many things she adored about Neil was that he could say no in such a way that she felt as if he was saying yes. It was like that when they went shopping for a couch too. He vetoed her first and second choices before they agreed on the final one, and although she was a little frustrated, it was something about his delivery, his pure heart, his sweet intention that made her want to cooperate. He was never harsh or scolding, his turn-downs seemed as pleasant as if they were in complete agreement. Consequently she didn't feel the urge to dig her heels in or insist on her way. Instead they laughed and got a kick out of discovering what might strike both their fancies.

Sweethearts are not always in sync, lovers don't always see eye to eye. She may have her heart set on a white chenille couch; he may prefer brown leather. She may want to make love; he may need to sleep. Differences and preferences do not matter as much as how you treat each other in the process of figuring out where you do agree. As the saying goes, "You can catch more flies with honey than with vinegar."

LOVE LESSON

1. Deliver preferences tenderly. Use your best positive, upbeat tone and add a little humor. "Oh, Sweetie, can we try that another time?"

2. Find an agreeable starting point, and continue from there. Think about this: You may not always be in sync about making love, but you probably can agree that you'd like to be. You may not agree on the color of the couch, but you can agree that you want a new one. A good starting point is agreeing that you'd like to agree.

3. Remember the saying: "You can catch more flies with honey than with vinegar." Use that approach in all your interactions.

4. Show enthusiasm. Your partner's preferences are as significant and as interesting as yours. Don't allow personal preferences to come between you; instead enjoy discovering what you can agree on.

5. Be creative. Put your individual likes and dislikes in the creative mixing bowl and see what concoction you come up with.

SAY YES AS OFTEN AS POSSIBLE

I once gave a 37-year-old man the assignment to buy flowers for his wife. I knew she would like to receive flowers because she had mentioned this several times in our joint sessions. Flowers are symbols of affection. Flowers send the message "You're special to me," and that gesture might give her the boost she needed.

The young man agreed to do the assignment, and when he arrived for our next session I was eager to hear the recap. You can probably guess where this story is headed: he didn't do the assignment.

"What?" I said, surprised, "You didn't buy flowers?"

"I forgot," he said with a shrug.

"You forgot?"

"Well, I forgot, but then when I did remember, I didn't know where to buy flowers," he stammered. "Besides, it was too late and I didn't know what kind she'd want anyway."

I was flabbergasted. A man his age, married six years, didn't know where to buy flowers or what kind of flowers his wife might enjoy? Was he being stubborn? Was he preoccupied with work or other obligations? What was the big deal about buying flowers, I thought. Was he rebelling? Maybe he was refusing to give because he was feeling unappreciated too.

When couples in counseling ignore my suggestions, I pay attention to the message behind their resistance. Shunning suggestions may be an indication that they've been resisting each other too. I didn't want to project my ideas onto him, but since I couldn't read his mind, I needed him to tell me what was going on. I don't like to make assumptions, but I decided it was worth the gamble and said to him, "There's a name for your excuses—it's called resistance." I suggested that if he could articulate a deeper explanation for his resistance we might be able to make some headway in getting his relationship back on track.

When the couple returned the following week, he acknowledged his tendency to resist whatever his wife suggested. If she wanted to try a restaurant across town, he had reasons why he didn't want to drive that far. If she wanted to see a documentary or a foreign film, he objected. When she asked if he would take dance lessons with their mutual friends, he agreed, but when the time came he threw up so many roadblocks that they missed registration.

His pattern of passive resistance was jeopardizing their relationship, and he knew that his objections had nothing to do with the restaurants, the movies, or the lessons. His opposition arose from something deeper.

I discovered that, as a young boy, he had had no voice in the matters that affected him. His father was critical and made fun of whatever he wanted to try. The only way he could speak up was by not cooperating. With this new awareness, he was able to break the pattern. The following week he not only gave his wife the flowers she'd been craving but he also brought her a chocolate bar and a jar of peanut butter. Turns out that her guilty treat is dipping a square of chocolate into peanut butter. Such a little gesture left them both encouraged that they could work their problems through.

LOVE LESSON

1. Let your sweetheart teach you. It is very likely that one element of your attraction was the fact that you both have things to teach each other. From the conscious (she's a good tennis player and you want to get better; he's a master gardener and you've always wanted to grow vegetables in your backyard) to the subconscious (we are attracted to people who somehow bring our unresolved childhood issues to the surface), chances are your partner has much to show you about yourself and the world. What can you learn from your lover today?

2. Expand your world. If you're stuck in a rut of resisting, if you are cutting off your nose to spite your face, then please be honest about it. Giving excuses for reasons why you don't want to try something new limits who you are and puts a damper on the experiences you and your partner could be sharing.

3. Say yes as often as possible. Resistance is a downer and dampens happiness. A healthy balance means plenty of yeses sprinkled with a few well-chosen nos. Use nos for situations that are destructive. Say no directly.

4. Take a small action. If buying a woman flowers or holding her hand or cleaning the kitchen counter eases her day or brings her a moment of feeling cared for, then do it. If ironing a man's shirts, fixing his breakfast, or sitting next to him while he reads the paper brings him comfort, do it. These simple acts provide equilibrium for hectic days and soothe defeated spirits.

5. Step out of your comfort zone. Your partner wants the best for you. If he is making a suggestion or a request, if she is prodding you out of your comfort zone, it might be good for you to try it.

CHECK IN

Every morning—even when she is in a hurry—Libby asks Martin what he will be doing that day. His answers vary: "Playing racquetball after work," or "Making a presentation to upper management," or "Have a meeting with the staff." Then Martin pauses, kisses Libby, and asks the same question: "What does your day look like, baby?"

Connection is fueled by check-ins. Knowing what your sweetheart is dealing with each day helps you both feel less alone in the big wide world. When you hear about her demands, the unexpected setbacks, the hurdles he is about to tackle, you gain even more admiration for your partner's skill and determination. Checking in, like a shot of energy, is often the exact remedy needed to manage the daily grind. Just a simple question like "What does your day look like, baby?" is enough to motivate and cheer each other on.

When Jacquie asks Gary about his day he often answers, "Same old, same old."

Jacquie doesn't take that as his final answer, though. "Humor me, honey," she says, "You know I like details." It's the playful tone in her voice that makes her questioning so endearing.

Can't resist her, Gary thinks, as he gives her a brief account of his agenda. He teases her too about needing to know his every move, but she knows and he knows that daily check-ins are another way of saying "I care about you."

LOVE LESSON

1. Check in. Find out at least one thing that your partner will be doing and dealing with during the day. Don't assume you already know. Ask directly: "Honey, what's going on for you today?"

2. Check in on the go. Don't let check-ins slip through the cracks. Don't take phone calls or text messages for granted. These are quick ways of checking in. Such contacts let you know that someone is thinking of you and may be an indication that your partner needs reassurance from you.

3. Ask: "Is there anything I can do to make your day go smoother?" If your partner doesn't have an answer, notice what might be helpful and do that.

4. Stay in touch. Make an effort to keep in touch when you are away, when you are unusually busy, when your schedule is crammed, when you are running late. Send a message, leave a note, keep your honey informed. When there is a last-minute change of plans, fill your honey in on as much as possible.

5. Once in a while make an exceptional check-in. Turn an ordinary check-in into a memorable one. Give your sweetheart attention and make it distinctive. Write a love note and send it in the mail (not email), flirt, leave a risqué thought on the phone. That will make a mundane day exceptional, and besides, exchanging intimate thoughts increases the pulse.

CHAPTER VII

KISS, KISS, CUDDLE, CUDDLE

Being in a relationship is like attending
preschool and graduate school all at once.
Each week and each year
there is much to absorb and figure out.
Play is a fundamental part of the curriculum.
So please don't bypass fun and fooling around.
What will you learn?
Not to take yourself so seriously.
To laugh at your own foibles.
To lighten up.
To walk silly, talk silly, be silly,
to wiggle and giggle.
You will learn about the kiss, kiss
and the cuddle, cuddle.

GET COMFY WITH AFFECTION

We need affection to thrive. You may have heard those
horrendous stories of children left languishing for hours
in their cribs, alone, never touched or held. It takes years
to recover from such deprivation. Touch is our first meaningful connection to the world, the way we feel close and
safe. No matter how old we are, we never outgrow our
need for touch and physical closeness. Without touch we
sink inside ourselves.

Zeek grew up in a family of bear-huggers, hand-
holders, and cuddlers and married Mel, who came from
a family of stiff handshakers and arm's-length quick pat-
on-the-backers. The first time Zeek met his in-laws-to-
be it was a collision of cultures. "Nope, I'll have none of
that," Zeek said as he wrapped his arms around his future
mother-in-law. "I'm a hugger, not a shaker," he informed
his stiff future father-in-law. The family wasn't sure that
they liked his approach, but for the sake of their daughter
they obliged. It took Mel some time to get used to Zeek's
affectionate touches too. She liked his warmth, but all that
hugging, holding hands, smooching, and spooning was
foreign to her and sometimes her automatic reaction when
he reached for her was to pull away. To accept the pleasure
of his touch, she had to stop herself from cringing. She
took a deep breath and noticed the sensations of his fingers

running through her hair, gave attention to his cheek brushing hers, and absorbed the vibrations that rippled through her body as he wrapped his arms around her.

Affection warms the body and satisfies the spirit—it makes us feel almost invincible. Affection is the sweet connection that begins on the surface and reaches to the depths. We touch and feel contentment in our soul.

LOVE LESSON

1. Expand your repertoire. Try all of these techniques until you become an expert: neck kisses, butterfly kisses, lip locks, fingers entwined, hand-holding, hand squeezes, public smooches, winks, shoulder rubs, back rubs, hand rubs, gentle embraces, quick hugs, full-body hugs, teddy-bear hugs, lingering hugs, ear nibbles, ear whispers, foot massages, arm tickles, pillow talks, cuddles, spooning, eye-gazing, body-dancing, body rubs.

2. No pat-pat-pat. Back pats are for babies, not for lovers. Join with your sweetheart in an enfolding embrace that relays the warmth of your heart. Feel the tension leave as you tenderly snuggle into a long embrace.

3. Breathe deeply. Do not hold your breath. Have you noticed how many people hold their breath while hugging? A good hugger is a deep breather. Breathing deeply makes all the difference. It relaxes body and mind and revs up the energy moving between you.

4. Let your body be alive. Notice how your hand comes alive when someone touches it. Just a moment before that touch, you weren't even noticing your hand, but with that touch you suddenly feel a tingle. Isn't that fun? Touch is fun. Touch is healing. Touch boosts the immune system.

5. Melt. Experience ease. Merge. Drop your boundaries and take down your walls. Let your lover come close.

LIVE JUICY

Sex is not the thermometer of love. Lovemaking is not confined to 45 minutes of sex. It does not begin when the lights go out. Love play begins long before foreplay. And it is not confined to the bedroom. The way sweethearts treat each other, the daily acts of kindness, the loving glances, the genuine consideration, the mutual respect—it is this that empowers love. There are couples who make love like this all day and every day, and they may never need to have intercourse; and there are couples who never make love, even when they are engaging in intercourse.

You can have great sex without being in love. You can have great sex and go your separate ways. You can have no sex and be happily together. You can have poor sex and have a deep spiritual connection. Every couple has their own style, and there's a wide spectrum of normal. Some couples fight and have makeup sex, others live together joyfully without sex. There's a broad range in between.

Regardless of whether you are having a lot of sex or no sex, never ever let yourself go numb. Numbing is deadly for passion. There is no better feeling than to be alive, with your juices flowing. Love is full of energy, and you can become receptive to it because it is always there underneath the surface. Love energy is joyous, and joy is always linked to sexual feelings. What we call sex is but a small part of the love energy that relaxes the body, uplifts our spirit, and connects our souls. Developing the ability to look your partner in the eyes—not harshly or menacingly but softly, in a wide-eyed way—is tremendously effective in enhancing one's capacity for playful, joyful love energy. When we look into each other's eyes a deep exchange occurs, a mysterious osmosis.

LOVE LESSON

1. Live juicy. If you want to have good sex, do everything you can that gets you excited about your life. When you are interested in life, sex is joyful. When you are interested in sex, life is joyful. They go together.

2. Think of your sweetheart with affection throughout the day. Rise to the level where your thoughts are positive. Don't push yourself to think tender thoughts, but rather find the level inside you where thoughts of love and caring already exist.

3. Gaze. Try this: behold your lover up close, eye to eye, without holding your breath. While you do this, relax your face and shoulders. You'll soon discover, if you haven't yet, why the eyes have been called windows to the soul.

4. Consider deeper desires. We are conditioned to think we want sex or should want sex. Often we're not tuned in to the deeper part of us that wants something different. When we don't listen to ourselves, something goes wrong—a sort of dysfunction.

5. Look at it this way. Don't think of your sweetheart as doing something *to* you, think of your sweetheart as doing something *with* you.

BE A CAPSULE OF LOVE ENERGY

Chemistry, they say, is what attracts people to one another. That may be. But if, after the chemistry does its work, you don't rise to a higher level of awareness, the chemistry will eventually turn to resentment. The passion will still be there, but the attraction will become malicious and revengeful. That's what soap operas are based on, and a lot of literature. That's what a lot of people still call love.

Sex isn't about bodies seen from the outside; it's about your body experienced from the inside. The journey to ecstasy is inward. So don't be influenced by the subtle sexual propaganda the slick magazines sell; that's all just deftly veiled pornography and sophisticated teasing. You don't need to have a perfect body. You don't need to have a perfect anything. You can just be yourself. If you and your beloved are ready for meaningful, heart-moving contact, then decide together that you are going to create a fun little capsule of love energy as often as you can. How do you begin? You warmly hold your partner's hands, look steadily into his or her eyes, and smile! The smile is what does it. Creating this heartwarming island of love energy will reconnect you with your partner in a positive way.

What sex is really about is the magic of meeting the other person. Even with someone you have lived with for years there is always new energy to experience together.

Sex is the unexpected meeting in which one person gives everything—totally—that one human being can give to another. It is about nakedness and it is about mystery. It isn't about what you do together, it is about meeting—a meeting that transcends time, worry, and ambition. It is a moment of truth, an unforgettable glimpse of eternity. It is about the transcendence of all the usual parameters by which we relate. The more you try to hold on to your power, your influence, your opinions and status, the less likely it is that such magic will occur. Letting go of all those safeguards requires courage, of course, but the ultimate gift to yourself and your sweetheart is to disregard the obstacles and allow that miracle to transform you.

LOVE LESSON

1. Be a capsule of love energy. If you want to enhance sexual desire, move away from to-do lists and run toward whatever relaxes body, mind, and spirit. Stop thinking. Be aware of your body. In the comfort of a long-term relationship, amid the routine of the day-to-day grind, it can be easy to take each other for granted. If this sounds like you, consider the needs of your partner and make those needs your priority.

2. Ramp up the sensual. Chill the glasses on Monday, add a dimmer switch to the light in the bedroom on Tuesday, etc. Continue emphasizing sumptuous atmosphere through the weekend. Repeat each week until juicy energies are flowing. (If you get bored with all the sexual energy running through your veins, don't worry, you can always return to the habit of taking life seriously again.)

3. Have a chuckle. Someone once said, "If men are a microwave oven, woman are a slow-burning stove." Incorporate both styles of cooking.

4. Give and get. You know what they say about love and sex. It's like a magic penny—the more sex you give, the more love you get. The more love you give, the more sex you get.

5. Eliminate solemn and stern. Sex is not a serious subject. Important yes, serious no. A person who has a healthy interest in sex is not a serious person. Such a person may be lighthearted, loving, caring, tender, dedicated, good-natured, and playful, but not serious. Seriousness and lovemaking do not mix.

SHH!

Week after week, Sydney and Oliver sat in front of me for marriage counseling, but I seldom got a word in edgewise. They were busy convincing, complaining, analyzing, critiquing, and criticizing. Occasionally I tried to insert an observation or make a suggestion, but neither seemed to pay much attention to me. It was as if each of them was on a mission to win, debating for points. It looked as if they were having fun, but I suggested they might like to try another style of relating.

"Shh!" I said at the end of the fourth session. "Shh," I said as I put my finger in front of my lips. "Silence is very important for love. So I'm giving you an assignment this week. When the kids are asleep, turn off the television, computers, and phones and sit silently next to each other."

"For how long?" Oliver asked.

"Fifteen minutes." I said.

"Whoa!"

"How many times?" Sydney asked.

"Once every night."

"You're kidding!" they gasped in unison, as if what I suggested was outrageous.

"That'll be new." Seems they hadn't been silent that long in years.

If you've ever listened to the silence of the night, you know our deep interrelationship with the sky and stars. If you've ever sat silently holding hands, you know how a heart is stirred by a silent connection. Silence is full of energy, and that energy gets things moving in a sexy direction. Talking is only one way of relating. Words are the tools of the mind. Compassionate silence is a tool of the heart. If you can't sit quietly next to your sweetheart, you will miss out on a lot of tenderness and energy flowing between you.

While it's important to speak openly, honestly, and directly, too much talk becomes a barricade to closeness. According to John Gottman, a relationship expert at the University of Washington, most couples have the same problems and differences after 10, 20, even 30 years of marriage that they did when they first got together. Thus, you may never "resolve" your differences. The key to a successful relationship is not endless communication about differences, but remaining kind and respectful toward each other despite your differences.

LOVE LESSON

1. Say less. Choose words carefully. Before you speak, ask yourself if what you are about to say will enhance intimacy and boost energy, or squelch it.

2. Change the length of the conversation. Instead of talking about a hot subject for hours or days, as some couples do, shorten the conversation to 10 minutes. Instead of complaining using 20 sentences or a paragraph, state your concern in three short sentences. Few words are more effective than a bundle. Too many words become a lecture. Nobody wants to be lectured.

3. Love like a verb. That is to say, take action. We are not what we say, rather we are what we do. If you want to feel closer to your partner, don't start a conversation about your day at work, about your kids, or about a problem in your relationship. Instead, act like a verb. Smile, gaze, wink, touch, cuddle, and kiss.

4. Go on a silent date. Spend an evening together without saying a word, letting the unspoken energy flow between you and lead the way. Observe more. Start noticing the small details about your partner: the way his eyes look just before he is about to laugh, the shape of her fingers when she picks up a wine glass.

5. Have a lot more sex. Need I say more? Your partner doesn't need to understand everything about you to have great sex.

BE A ROMANTIC

If you're not inclined to write poetry or speak in flowery sentences, you can still be a romantic by encouraging your sweetheart. "Honey, you can do that" is a romantic sentence. We all need encouragement—you do, and so does your loved one. We're all helpless little people trying to deal with a complex world. The rules change practically every day and it's hard to keep up. In this fast-paced society full of daily frustrations and obligations, we need all the support, encouragement, and romance we can gather.

Romance without encouragement is shallow. I know men who bring flowers but never ask about their sweetheart's dreams. I know women who crave romance while discouraging their lover's hobbies and pastimes. I see parents who discourage and squelch their children in subtle ways—putting up roadblocks, complaining, and making the dream impossible. Discouragement adds up and is ultimately lethal. If your loved one has a dream, tell him it's a wonderful dream. Don't knock it. Don't cloud the dream with fear. Whatever she want to do, encourage her to go for it. Say, "Honey, I know you can do that."

"Your pies are perfection," Miguel told Mary. "Poetry in a crust" he called them, and said, "I know you could sell them." After years of romantic praise like that, Mary rented space in a commercial kitchen. Out of the gate, she sold two whipped chocolate tortes to a local restaurant, and two years later she has all the orders she can handle. "Miguel believed in me more than I believed in myself."

We all have more talents than we are using, so try to see what talents your loved ones have and tell them about their talents. Everyone is gifted in some way. Help your sweet ones see how they are special, how their gifts are unique. Take note of their accomplishments, however small.

LOVE LESSON

1. Use this formula: For an electrifying day, add a splash of the poetic with a dash of the practical. Stimulating days include both the poetic and the practical.

2. Encourage. If romance is fading, be generous with encouragement. Our inadequacies are relatively unimportant, and with encouragement we can overcome them. Encouragement fuels romance.

3. Grant dreams. Say often, "That's a wonderful dream." "You can do it." Ask, "How can I help your dream come true?"

4. Believe. Wholeheartedly support your loved ones' talents. When you believe in them, they believe in themselves.

5. Promote your own dreams. Advance your own vision. You have special talents too. Romantic intrigue is made up of dreams.

CHOOSE HAPPY

If your partner isn't happy, you will feel it. If you aren't happy, your partner will feel it. Happiness is both an inside job and a joint venture. If you want a happy, satisfied, fulfilled coupledom, here's the ABCD's of it.

A. Let your sweetie be true to herself. Do not try to squelch, change, muffle, edit, censor, morph, stifle, or push her to be anything other than the way she naturally is in hopes that she will become closer to your "ideal" mate. You must love your partner right now, for all that he is, "flaws" and all.

B. Be true to yourself. That means do not squelch, change, muffle, edit, censor, morph, stifle, or push yourself to be anything other than the way you naturally are in hopes of becoming something closer to your partner's "ideal" mate. Your partner must love you right now, for all that you are, "flaws" and all.

C. Grant yourself and your sweetheart permission to change. Just because your sweetheart had one idea, vision, or belief system when you first met doesn't mean he will still have that same idea, vision, or belief system one or two or 10 years down the road.

D. You will not be the same person you were before you fell in love. Your sweetheart will not be the same either. Perhaps you've heard yourself say, "But she's not the person I married." Or "He's different than he was when we first met." This is true. Each and every time we fall in love we step into the mix and are blended. We are muddled into a twosome, and with a little luck, lots of awareness, and plenty of hard work we emerge as a part of a delightful and rare concoction.

LOVE LESSON

1. Assess your partner's happiness. Ask yourself, Am I doing everything within my power to aid in my partner's happiness? Remember, if your partner is unhappy in the relationship, you too will be unhappy in the relationship.

2. Do both. Pursue your passions and reserve time for your sweetheart. Don't take your sweetheart or yourself for granted. Develop yourself and allow your partner the same freedom to evolve.

3. Develop a spiritual life. I am not talking about religious doctrine or church affiliation here, but about a recognition of something bigger than yourself, a realization that you are connected to those around you through the shared human condition, that you are a part of that which is eternal, divine, and true. How do you do this? By making a spiritual ritual part of daily practice. It doesn't need to be time-consuming, but it does need to occur regularly. Write down five things you are grateful for, say a prayer, meditate, or simply sit under the stars, look up at the moon, and contemplate the vastness of the universe.

4. Take care of your body. Move your body. Dance, ride a skateboard, ski, jump rope, walk, lift weights. It doesn't matter what you do, just so long as you do it. And do it daily. Our bodies are meant to move. Eat right. Eating right means eating lots of fresh fruits and vegetables, beans, organic and free-range meats, and whole grains. It means not overeating. It means not eating foods that are precooked and packaged. It means occasionally allowing yourself to indulge in your favorite dessert.

5. Develop your intellect. Read and think critically about topics outside your comfort zone on a regular basis. Find others who are eager to take part in intelligent discussion and friendly debate. We are social creatures. We cannot survive or be happy without the company of others. Be loving to all people, all creatures, all life that you come into contact with.

MELT. MERGE. DISSOLVE.

The highest moments in a relationship are the ones when the two of you merge and melt together, when you are not only on the same page, but on the same word, the same character, the same swooping slope of that soft, smooth letter *S*. Yes! Yes! Yes! You are simpatico. Those moments might last for minutes, hopefully for hours, eventually for days. When those moments happen naturally it feels like a magic dust has blessed your union. Most of the time, however, melting, merging, dissolving requires a concerted effort. Working at being simpatico may sound contrived and unromantic, but in truth, working at it is essential.

What is the secret to melting in each other's arms? What are the keys to feeling safe and cared for? Answer: Loving responses. Perspective. The ability to sidestep emotional chaos and reassure each other.

We all have a deep need to connect with another person. We all want to have a deep, meaningful, loving relationship. We want to know we can depend on our sweetheart to be there for us. This is natural. There is nothing wrong with needing love from your partner. Our sweetheart is the person who banishes our fears of not being lovable and having no one care about us. Our sweetheart proves that we do indeed matter.

"I know my dad and mom love each other," seven-year-old Mindy told me, "because when they get mad they are still nice." It is not easy to be nice in the heat of an argument when both of you are raw and vulnerable. But if you commit to striving for that goal, you can achieve it. Love is not a resting spot. Love is dynamic and turbulent. It is possible to love and be loved, but only if you are willing to experience the full range of what it means to be alive.

LOVE LESSON

1. Make the first move. Reach out. Hold her hand. Kiss his cheek. Cook her dinner. Massage her feet. Jump his bones. It is easy to be too measured, to let disagreements pile up, to keep score, to ruminate about the past, to analyze your partner's every move, to hold back until the "right moment" to lose yourself. But there is no right moment to melt, to merge, to dissolve. And there is no wrong moment either. This is the moment. Let go of your ego. Let go of your fears. Let go of the past. Don't calculate whose "turn" it is to show a loving gesture. Strategy has no place when it comes to authentic connection. So make your loving move now.

2. Say no sparingly. *No* blocks the flow of energy. If you say no to your partner, make sure to follow it up with a yes of some sort.

3. Say yes frequently. Let every cell in your body exclaim, Yes! Even if you aren't feeling 100 percent certain, say yes anyway. Melting requires openness and commitment. You cannot melt if you are closed and wishy-washy.

4. Come together as "we." You are one person, an "I." Your sweetheart is one person, an "I." But when the two of you come to a place of agreement you are simpatico, a "we." To find agreement, hold a conversation. Include these sentences: "How can we work this out?" "We will work it out." "We are working together."

5. Wait expectantly. Sometimes the process of melting happens instantaneously, but usually it happens slowly after you've developed a trusting bond. Melting also ebbs and flows; you melt together, you drift apart; you melt together; you drift apart. You come back.

CHAPTER VIII

A REWARDING VICIOUS CIRCLE

Trust that you are lovable,
even when there is no
apparent evidence that you are.
You are lovable
even with your limitations.
Accepting limitations
does not diminish lovableness.
It is the opposite.
When we make peace with our limitations
we become more lovable, and
as we become more lovable
we become more loving toward others,
and then we become even more lovable.
This is one of the most
rewarding
vicious circles
we can fall into.

TELL THE TRUTH OF THE MOMENT

When Scott and Olivia first became an item they did everything together, told each other everything, agreed on issues, and thought alike. Togetherness was fun; besides, there was so much security in being a "we" that neither wanted to rock the love boat by mentioning differing thoughts or unpleasant feelings. Neither wanted to mention the loneliness and boredom they sometimes felt. Scott didn't mention that he dreaded grocery shopping and Olivia never said directly that she didn't want to attend his soccer games every Sunday. Underneath the security and thrill was a pang of angst that neither admitted. They were afraid that the truth would be too hurtful, so they kept it quiet, and that caused considerable confusion.

There is an old adage: The truth will set you free. This applies in relationships too. The truth of the moment clarifies unspoken wishes, relieves underlying tensions, and alleviates any passive-aggressive tendencies and manipulation. No double messages or reading between the lines. Sitting across from Scott at their favorite neighborhood bistro, discussing which gym they would join and their workout schedules, Olivia surprised herself by blurting the truth out loud: "I want to go to the gym by myself." She didn't know all the reasons, only that she felt the urge— so, instinctively, she spoke the truth of her situation. "I need alone time to think and I do my best thinking in the gym."

Scott argued that it made sense to drive to the gym together and grab a bite afterward. "Besides, we aren't talking when we're at the gym," he said.

He almost convinced her that she was being foolish, but she persisted. "I want to go to the gym by myself."

It took some getting used to, but it wasn't long before Scott could acknowledge it. "I didn't like the idea at first, but now I appreciate not having to coordinate my workout with hers."

The simple truth has potential to revitalize the energy between you. Being a vibrant couple doesn't mean hanging out in each other's back pocket 24/7. There's a time to be together and a time to be apart. Just as gaps between the notes shape the beauty of the music, gaps infuse affection and delight, tenderness and passion, in togetherness.

It's liberating to acknowledge the plain truth of a situation: "Right now, I'm lonely," "Right now, we're going through a rough patch." "Right now, I'm discouraged." "Right now, I want to go alone." The plain truth is simply that: the truth of this moment, right now. The plain truth says nothing about the next moment, the next day, or the next year. The plain truth is about this moment, the moment you are in right now.

LOVE LESSON

1. Acknowledge the plain and simple truth of the moment. The simple truth in this moment may or may not be the truth in the next moment, the next hour, the next week, or the next year.

2. Consider: What is true for me today? What do I need right now? Let the truth rise in you. Sit with it. Speak it.

3. Begin with: "Right now." "Right now, I am thinking
   _____."
   "Right now, I am feeling_____."
   "Right now, I would like_____."
   Notice the peace of mind and new energy that simple truth brings.

4. Enjoy gaps. Some experts say that gaps in togetherness add mystery and fuel desire. So if your partner says, "Right now, I want to spend time alone," it is probably not a permanent condition.

5. Listen for the truth of the moment. Encourage your partner to tell the truth of the situation. You won't have to wonder anymore. The truth can set you free. Hooray for that.

USE THE CONVERSATION TOOLBOX

I once attended a wedding where the officiator began the ceremony with "Dearly beloved: We are gathered here today to help each other get through life." Isn't it wonderful that we can lend a hand and be of assistance to each other? On that note, I would like to extend a helping hand and offer you my conversation toolbox: phrases that will make your heart-to-hearts easier and sweeter. Memorize and use often.

"Let's think that over."

"Help me understand."

"Tell me more."

"What are you going to do?"

"Is there anything you would like me to do?"

"Sweetie, how can I help?"

"Let me do that for you."

"You take it easy."

"Come sit by me."

"I want a happy life and a good relationship with you."

"Let's make it happen."

"I see your point of view."

"You might be right."

"I could be wrong."

"I've been wrong before."

"We both could be right."

"It's nice to see you, honey."

"I love you."

"I miss you."

"I'm glad we are figuring this out."

"Yes, we can do that."

Words have power to wound or heal, inspire or defeat. They can tear us down or lift our spirits. Words alter our perceptions and influence our feelings. We enhance our connection by the words we use.

LOVE LESSON

1. Memorize affirming phrases. Use them frequently. They add zest and generate enthusiasm and cooperation. Positive words point in a positive direction.

2. Increase your vocabulary. Add both romantic words and comforting words to your conversation toolbox. Just as we need romantic words to feel excited, we need comforting words to feel safe.

3. Watch your tone. Never let fear or negativity drive your conversation. Keep the tone of your voice mellow. When speechless, say, "Honey, I'd like to think this over and get back to you."

4. Have high hopes. Use words of inspiration, hold the belief that dreams do come true, that anything is possible. Think buoyant thoughts and express those expectant thoughts out loud.

5. Be generous. Use love names and terms of endearment often. Praise the simplest acts. Say please and thank you. Tell the people you love that you love them.

FAKE IT

Regardless of what they are feeling inside, Belina and Elon have developed the ability to fake it. After what they've been through and what they survived, they operate from an attitude of gratitude. Belina is optimistic by nature and prefers gratitude over ruminating about what is wrong, what could go wrong, or what did go wrong. Elon holds a realistic view and can be pessimistic, but when life is difficult, which it has been for them, they stand beside each other and lift each other up. When one is glum or devastated the other bears the pain and fakes it. That's right, when things are bleak, they fake it for each other.

When their daughter was born with a birth defect they were told she might not live, and if she did, her legs might be paralyzed. The baby needed immediate surgery and would need many more. Belina and Elon were heartbroken. They cried together, cried alone, held on to each other and pulled each other up. If Belina had a meltdown, Elon took charge. If Elon was overcome by grief, Belina stepped in to question the doctors. When one felt weak, the other acted strong. When one could only see what was going wrong, the other focused on what was going right. During the bleakest moments, when a good outcome seemed unlikely, they faked it, acted as if something good was coming, no matter what they were thinking or feeling inside.

That's the faith couples impart. When you are unsure how you will survive the difficulties you're facing, one speaks of hope so the other can hold on. One acts as if the problem is handled so the other can believe that everything will be all right. When one is weak, the other is strong. When one gives up, the other carries on. Leaning on each other, they become strong. One acts as if there is light at the end of the tunnel and the other sees the glimmer.

LOVE LESSON

1. Fake it. When you're down in the dumps and your partner down further, fake it. Pretend that you've got it handled. Say, "Honey, everything will be all right."

2. Act as if. Act as if you believe that there is hope, and you will begin to believe that indeed there is. This will give your sweetheart hope too. That hopeful combination has the power to actually make things better. Say, "Good things are coming our way."

3. Keep the faith. Imagine things getting better. Imagine bad turning good. Speak encouragement. Take turns saying to each other: "We can do this, we are doing this, we will get through." Regardless of your troubles, commit to being constructive.

4. Lean together. Lean together and you both will be stronger.

5. Try this. "I fake it till I make it, and I act as if I am making it, and guess what? I am making it."

TALK ABOUT MONEY WITHOUT GETTING HEATED

Here's the bottom line on relationship money matters: It doesn't matter how much money you have or don't have if you can't agree on how to spend it. "I don't mind living on a budget," she says, "as long as I can spend what I want."

Art is a spender. Sadie is a saver. Art wants to take a vacation at a sunny resort; Sadie wants to buy a tent and sleeping bags and go hiking on vacations. Art wants to dine out with friends at the new restaurant; Sadie would rather invite everyone over for a potluck. Art talks about buying a new car, and Sadie rolls her eyes. Sadie suggests he ride the bus to work as she does, and Art rolls his eyes. Is there hope for a couple with differing ideas about money management?

Like most disagreements that arise, it isn't the fact that you have different financial agendas that makes or breaks your relationship, but rather the way you deal with those differences. Can you talk about hot subjects without getting heated? "Sweetie, do you think you and I have the same ideas about money?" Zoey asked. No need to come up with a solution or meet on the same page right away. The first conversation is not the time to debate or try to convince your partner that your views are "right." The initial discussions are for brainstorming and sharing viewpoints. Money differences often arise from differing lifestyle ideals and core values. Start with questions such as these: Are my daily spending habits in sync with my deepest core values? What secret dreams am I squelching? What do I want my legacy to be when I leave this planet?

Financial struggles are tough, and talking about them is tricky. Having too little can be disastrous. Conversely, so can having too much. If you are preoccupied with money and possessions, you won't experience joy as you might if you were focused on joy instead. When you compare your situation to the neighbors' you may feel cocky or defeated. How much the neighbors have or don't have has nothing to do with how happy you can be. Zoey's motto is: spend less, consume less, kiss more. Your relationship in and of itself, not your possessions, is a source of joy, excitement, and comfort.

LOVE LESSON

1. Spend below your means. You cannot live in healthy balance if you are stressed about money. Save more than you spend. Do not become dependent on activities that require you to consume goods or spend money to have fun and feel connected. If you are, that's a signal that your relationship is in need of attention.

2. Talk without getting heated. Practice discipline in your speech and spending habits. Set limits for yourself. Create a budget and spend only what you agree upon. Say no to things that will stretch you beyond your financial means. While not everything will be in balance, in equal measure, all of the time, a stable financial balance is a worthy pursuit.

3. Take financial ownership together. No money secrets allowed. Make sure that you are both informed about your financial standing. Share equally the responsibility for managing the bills. If one of you writes the checks to pay the bills, let the other keep the financial files in order.

4. Establish "Yours," "Mine," and "Ours" accounts. Contribute to a joint account for the family necessities and for future savings. Keep the remainder in separate accounts. That way you can spend or save some money as you please without a discussion over every penny.

5. Have more sex. Living below your means inspires better sex than fighting over bills you can't pay. It's so true.

CALL FOR A WORK-AROUND

A work-around is a creative fix to what, at first glance, might seem like an impasse. It's a twist that sidesteps a potential standoff, an outside-the-box revelation that keeps rapport lively and the tone upbeat. With an attitude of "let's see what's possible," collaboration is infused with excitement and trust. That's because if two heads are better than one, two hearts are even better.

Marv and Holly put their heads together and came up with 11 work-arounds for the gridlock that had been holding them back. Every Sunday morning it was the same thing—Marv was turned on and ready to make love. Holly felt torn because the children were frantic and wanting breakfast. For months, he's been prodding her to arrange for someone to look after the kids on Sunday morning, but she says, "Don't be silly, Marv, I couldn't make love to you with a stranger in the house!"

"Look," he says, "we're entitled to a little privacy. We have needs too. There's got to be one day in the week when we can make love without hurrying."

By the way, when you've reached an impasse, don't let your lover see you sweat. Stay cool. Don't react. Don't bite. When tensions get sticky, do whatever it takes to stay unruffled.

Work-arounds are sculpted over time and Marv and

Holly devised theirs like so: Number 1: a lock and a "do not disturb" sign for the bedroom door. Number 2: the kids are spending the night at Grandma's. Number 3: the kids have early swimming lessons and the neighbor is driving. Number 11: Mommy and Daddy are taking a bath, get your own cereal.

Work-arounds are created as needed. What was invigorating last year may not be exciting this year. What you enjoyed last month may not interest you now. What captivated you at 20 may not at 40. That's where the thrill comes from—he changes and she changes and suddenly there's pleasure in getting reacquainted. A work-around, by the way, is not coercion or manipulation, it's two people enjoying the process of working together. The simple phrase "Honey, this calls for a work-around" is recognition that even though you might not agree or get exactly what you thought you wanted, it's stimulating to figure out how to overcome the predicament.

LOVE LESSON

1. Concoct a work-around. Put your heads and hearts together and see what magic you two geniuses can dream up. Wink and say: "Honey, this calls for a work-around."

2. Liven up. Doing the same old things the same old way is boring. In a rut? Live artistically. Liven up and let the juices flow.

3. Be resourceful. Don't imagine that there's no way out of your situation. Don't let negativity bog you down. No matter what is going on, the quality of your day depends on one factor: your imaginative responses.

4. Be innovative. Don't accept relationship snags as a permanent condition. Work around them.

5. Pat yourselves on the back. Believe in your own genius. Believe in the genius of your partner. Say, "My goodness, honey, we are geniuses."

BE TRUSTWORTHY

To love and be loved is wonderful. Even if there are problems, love brings tremendous joy. Love makes the day fresh and exciting. You're alive and everything is suddenly more *up* and you look forward to things that a while back were drudgery. When you don't have love you go around sulking and looking for it. You feel desperate. But now you have it. You really wanted love and now you have it. Rejoice! Be happy.

Pay attention, appreciate the people who love you, be trustworthy. Trust expands when we do what we say we will do, when you say you'll be home by seven and are home by seven. Trust can be broken with a broken promise. Be joyful and thankful every day because love is the most sought after experience in the whole world. I know people seek money and are impressed with power, but I will tell you a secret—they are really looking for love, whether they know it or not. Love is more precious than gold, more prized than diamonds, goes deeper and spreads wider than wealth. Love has nothing to do with who earns the most money. If you have love and a small bank account you are richer than the person with a big bank account and no love. I have sat with the dying and I have never heard a dying person wish that they had earned more money. If they have any regrets, it is that they wished they had been more loving.

In going about your day it's easy to get distracted from your real purpose: wanting to make your sweetheart's life a little easier. Picking up the slack when times are tough, seeing what your partner needs and taking care of it. Don't wait for him or her to ask, don't wait until things get really bad, don't wait until your partner is severely stressed, depressed, or sick before jumping in and offering to help. Sooner or later one of you will have to go to work and one of you will have to do the laundry, but daily duties must never overshadow love. A trustworthy lover is certain about that.

LOVE LESSON

1. Be more loving. Really. It is that simple. A trustworthy lover is loving.

2. Be happy. When you find yourself feeling disgruntled, imagine turning your relationship into a romantic comedy. You can make a drama into a comedy by a slight shift in emphasis. Image yourself the director of each scene. When you go through the day thinking of your life this way, you'll get distance and perspective that will make you laugh out loud. Life is full of absurdity and ridiculousness. If you are serious you will miss it all.

3. Be amazed. Be intrigued and curious about your partner's body, mind, and spirit. Approach your partner with an attitude of "What new thing can I learn about you today?" Even if you have been together for 30 years, there is always something new to learn, a new question to ask, a new way to touch, a new feeling to share. Be fresh. Be open. Be excited. Be prepared to be surprised.

4. Fixate on positives. See the best in your sweetheart. Look at the things you love and ignore the little things that annoy and irritate you.

5. Do favors. When you extend a helping hand, offer a kind word, and do little favors, troubles are bearable.

ACCEPT

Have you ever dismissed a compliment by thinking, That's not true? or by saying, "I'm actually stupid, boring, ugly"? We have all done that—whether consciously or subconsciously, many of us believe that we are unlovable. It is sad that we are given so many reasons to hate ourselves: not rich enough, not smart enough, not attractive enough, not famous enough, just simply not good enough. When we believe that we are not good enough we try to prove that we are unlovable by denying, belittling, dismissing, or ignoring anybody who expresses love toward us.

Gianna and Abe spend hours together, go on adventures together, share their most secret secrets. They are close friends who care about each other, and although they are not married, essentially they are family. In spite of this, whenever Abe says to Gianna, "I love you," she cringes and responds with a curt "No, you don't." It's hard for her to receive love or to believe that anyone could love her. This confuses Abe. Whenever Gianna rejects his loving gestures he takes a step back and wonders what he did wrong. Gianna is not a perfect person, and neither is Abe. None of us are. We all have flaws and we are all still worthy of love despite those flaws. We may want the perfect partner, we may want to be the perfect partner, but we don't need perfection for love.

Accepting love is good for us. By accepting love we are not only doing something good for ourselves, we are doing something good for the person who loves us. Because the only thing better than receiving love is watching somebody delight in the love they have given.

LOVE LESSON

1. Soften yourself. Literally. You cannot accept love if you are holding your body tightly. Let all your muscles—from your jaw to your toes—relax, and your heart (which is a muscle too, remember) will be ready to accept love as it is given.

2. Soak it up. When somebody says, "I love you," breathe, slow down, and soak up the meaning behind those words. Sigh, "Ohhh."

3. Hold your body open and ready to receive love. Most of us walk around with what I call "modern caveman posture." You know the look: hunched shoulders, dropped chin, eyes looking toward the ground. It comes from spending too much time in front of our computer screens and handheld devices. Modern caveman posture collapses the chest and keeps your heart shut off. Your body simply cannot receive love when you've got posture like this, so open your body and your heart by rolling your shoulders back, raising your chin up, and bringing your eyes forward.

4. Welcome acts of love. Everybody expresses love differently. Some people give compliments, some write eloquent love letters, some cuddle, some perform practical acts like vacuuming your car while you are away at work. Learn to interpret how your loved ones express their love for you. Accept those gestures.

5. Absorb. When love is given, you don't need to respond or reciprocate immediately. Let love soak in first before taking action. If you move too quickly, the impact of the loving act will likely be dampened. If you feel the need to respond, a simple "thank you" is perfect.

CHAPTER IX

ALL FOR THE BETTER

Although love may change us,
and although we may
change for love,
these changes must always be
for the better.
True love does not
squelch the other;
true love lifts both the lover
and the beloved closer to
their delightfully humble, lively,
magnificent selves.

PART IN LOVE

The path of love is unpredictable. Love carries our hearts places we never expected. Take this love story as an example: Peter and Chloe lived together for three and a half years. They're adorable. Not only do they love each other, they like each other. You can feel the vibe of caring and passion between them. The first year, certain they would be a couple forever, they rented a small house on an acre of land and started a garden. The next year, they expanded the family to include two dogs, one cat, goats, and chickens. The third year, they pooled their resources to buy the property even though it meant living on a tight, tight budget.

Things were progressing smoothly until an unexpected windfall knocked them for a loop. Peter got a promotion, which meant they would no longer be strapped for money. Inspired by the possibilities, he looked forward to supporting Chloe in style. Success was in the making. One month later Chloe landed her own dream job—the one she never thought she'd get—in Paris. She was ecstatic about moving to Paris and working in the fashion industry. Peter was not. Suddenly the disparity in their dreams—that they once hoped could be handled through compromise—became glaringly apparent.

Peter thrived on country living and was ready to be a

father. Chloe fancied herself in a quaint apartment, walking city streets, riding the Metro, sitting in bistros, studying art, and speaking French. She wasn't ready for children and not sure if she ever would be. The wind was blowing them in opposite directions. In an attempt to find a solution they came to counseling to discuss the various scenarios.

"We can live in Paris when we retire," Peter proposed in earnest. "We can travel there every year."

"We can own a farm when we retire," Chloe countered. "Maybe buy one in the south of France someday."

I had the honor to bear witness to their dilemmas, their honesty, and how meticulously they talked the options through. Should one set aside a dream to stay together? If one let go would resentment and guilt take hold? Were they selfish not to give what the other longed for? Had they never truly loved each other? These were difficult and heartrending discussions. No matter what solutions Peter and Chloe came up with, there would be ramifications. How does one decide when facing the loss of a dream versus the loss of a sweetheart? It might surprise you to know that as they weighed the options and cried about what they were facing, they grew closer and love grew. That's how openhearted love works. When you are open to hearing your beloved's dreams, when you're open to supporting those dreams—even if those dreams may cause your heart to break a little—love expands and brings you closer. Chloe and Peter came away from counseling wanting the best for each other.

Eventually, Chloe moved to Paris with the idea of checking it out for a year. After 19 months she was still there. Peter was living on his land, successful at his job, and ready to start a family. The last time I spoke with him, he and Chloe were meeting in New York to say another round of goodbyes. He had decided that he was ready to move on.

When you love a man, when you love a woman, the moment to part will come. Such is the nature of life. We part from all we love. If you are angry, unwilling, nasty, mean, destructive, aggressive, hateful, or full of revenge, if you set out to make your sweetheart miserable, if you try to hold on and convince your partner to stay, you have not loved at all. If you want the best for them, if you want them to be free to find what they are searching for, you will wish them well. You will be grateful. You will part in love and in gratitude for all they brought to your life.

We do not control the direction of the wind. We never know when parting will come. And so, dear reader, when you are with your beloved, love them totally. Love them every single hour of every single day. If you love totally, love will blossom in you and make you whatever you are becoming. You will part in love.

LOVE LESSON

1. Welcome love in all its forms. The capacity to love is directly related to our response to what life brings our way.

2. Be vulnerable. Share openly. Although you may be headed in opposite directions, being open and honest will bring you closer.

3. Hear. What is one small or large piece of information or truth that you would like your sweetheart to hear? Being heard is vital for emotional intimacy. Is there something your partner has been trying to tell you that you have not heard?

4. Be gentle in your response. When your sweetheart discloses something that stings or scares you, be careful about your reaction. If you freak out, it will shut off the possibility of more closeness and greater understanding.

5. Part with love. If and when the time comes to go your separate ways, be grateful for what love has taught you. Wish your sweetheart well.

KEEP YOUR EYES ON THE PRIZE

Bobbie loves love. She likes movies, books, soap operas, anything that has to do with romance. She dreams of writing a romantic novel, and at the rate she's reading, I am certain she will. She belongs to a book club that mails a new book each month. She tucks two or three into her backpack and reads where ever she is—at the bus stop, the hairdresser, getting her nails done, at her niece's gymnastic tryouts, sitting beside her husband, Will, at the baseball game. "I'm studying plot lines," she says when friends tease her about her paperback addiction. "I need to understand what makes the heroine tick, what makes a hero mysteriously charming." The ups and downs of relationships intrigue her. "You can't have love without drama," she says. Bobbie is enamored with the pursuit, the waiting, the surprise, the heartbreak, the tension, the candlelight, the dialogue, the glances, the agony, the riding off into the sunset, and the happy-ever-after ending.

While we certainly applaud Bobbie's focused attention in pursuing her dream of becoming a romance writer, there are concerns. Perhaps you can guess what those might be? Bobbie pines for the romance she reads about. Her husband is not the hero she fantasizes about. "He is a hard worker and loyal," she says, "but he isn't romantic."

Pursuit, rescue, adventure, being swept away are main

plots in movies and novels, but a steady dose distorts the reality and riches that mature love offers. There's nothing wrong with romance and nothing wrong with wanting a taste, but if movie screen characters are your role models, you'll get sidetracked and misinformed. There is not one formula for achieving happy-ever-after love. There are infinite ways to relate, to love, and be happy. There are thousands of ways to stimulate romance. Don't let fantasy cloud your vision. Romance lies in being open to the unexpected, in discovering something new about each other.

LOVE LESSON

1. Keep your eyes on the prize. Just as you must never compare your one-of-a-kind self to another, you must never compare your one-of-a-kind relationship to novels, movies, or fantasy. Blow kisses to the hero or heroine you've already got.

2. Spice it up. Do not get hooked on daydreams, soap operas, or sentimental love. Bring out your romantic side. Start by giving compliments. Throw in racy suggestions. Wear clean clothes.

3. Beware of pseudolove. Where do your ideas of love and romance come from? Be aware of what amusements, pastimes, and entertainments inform your outlook and choices. What you look at, hear, read, and talk about influences you. Don't allow pseudolove to detract you from pursuing the authentic.

4. Add anticipation. Do not live vicariously through others. Engaging in others' imaginary love dramas is a signal that you could benefit from finding excitement in your own. Buy tickets to a symphony and take your sweetie. Let the music move you, talk in whispers.

5. Create an occasion. Do not get stuck on past love or daydream about possible future love objects. Change the mood. Float balloons, blow bubbles, rearrange the furniture, move the mattress to the floor and sleep in front of the fireplace.

COOK FOR COMFORT

Do you feel anxious, out of sorts, or uneasy and you're not sure why? Do you look to your partner for reassurance? Are you disappointed when he doesn't understand what you need? Does that create dissension? If you answered yes to these questions, you are not alone. The chances are high that your partner is anxious and apprehensive at the same time you are. That's because when one person is upset, the other person feels it and becomes upset too.

Reid is concerned when he sees the look on Molly's face that indicates she's upset about something. When he asks what's wrong, she brushes him off with a snippy short answer, and that sets in motion a ripple of upset. Molly's upset triggers Reid's upset and the upset in the air multiplies. Reid worries that he has done something wrong. Both are distressed. Both need comfort. Reid zones out in front of the television while Molly distracts herself by frantically cleaning. They are polite, distant, agitated, and comfort deprived. That was before they discovered cooking.

After Reid and Molly took cooking classes together, they discovered that sometimes it's better to cook away your troubles than talk about them. Cooking and eating together sends the message "Everything will be all right" and "I am here for you." On weekends they decide on the menus for the coming week. No matter what upset they may be dealing with, chopping and dicing cheers them both up. Mixing ingredients is soothing and settles their nerves. After they've eaten, they feel better. By satisfying their bodies on the most basic level, they are empowered to face and handle whatever challenges life brings their way.

It is never wrong to reach out, reassure, and comfort your partner. If the vibe in the room is tense, that's a signal that you both need comforting. Whether it's a tiny disappointment festering or big trouble brewing, you can't effectively address the issues while distressed. Reassuring and comforting is always better than doing nothing. When in doubt about what to do, put on music, pull out a cookbook, plan menus, choose a recipe, chop, dice, cook, eat, feel better.

LOVE LESSON

1. Identify upset. Answer these questions. How do you recognize when you are upset? How do you recognize when your partner is upset?

2. Add comfort. Answer these questions: How do you comfort yourself? How do you comfort your partner? How does your partner comfort you? Add comfort to your daily routine.

3. Chop, cook, eat. You can never go wrong comforting each other with good comfort food. Instead of withdrawing, get out a cookbook. Instead of freaking out or zoning out, go to the kitchen and cook something delicious.

4. Say, "Everything will be all right." Say it as if you believe it. Trade tender, reassuring hugs. Discuss a plan to deal with upset. Some of our upsets are imagined, some are real, and both types benefit from reassurance.

5. Be a comfort leader. I know it is hard and unfair that you are called on to comfort others when you could use some comforting too, but that is exactly what a leader does. If you are upset, your partner is upset too. If Mom or Dad is upset, the children are upset, and vice versa. Everybody needs comforting. Step forward and be the comfort leader. Reassure those around you, and when you've comforted them, be sure to comfort yourself too.

FIND A PRIVATE CORNER

By the time Carla arrived for her first appointment, she was fantasizing about living on her own in a small apartment. "I want my own closet, my own bed, my own furniture, I want to listen to the music I like, eat organic, paint walls bright colors, I want a cat," she said. "I love my husband but I am always compromising." Carla had gone from her parents' home to a college dorm to marriage. She regretted not living on her own first and felt guilty and selfish for thinking this way. "Is it even possible to merge while maintaining individuality?" Carla wondered aloud. "Or is it a contradiction that leads to irresolvable frustration or ends in heartache?" That's a universal struggle: the paradox between wanting to be together and wanting to be alone, the tussle between compromise and being true to yourself. Carla instinctively knew that she needed to do something for herself because not doing so was leading to relationship burnout.

We are, all of us, on an individual journey to develop and follow our dreams. It's a journey that doesn't stop just because we are a sweetheart, a parent, have a career, and are in love. A relationship is not the end to a separate identity but an opportunity to expand our repertoire and broaden the definition of ourselves.

So how does one begin to manage the inner tug-of-war between being an individual and being a couple? Is it possible to be a private person and available for your sweetheart too? How do you balance personal desires with couple needs? Carla stayed with her husband and turned the large space behind the stairs into her private retreat, a hideaway complete with a big cozy chair and a hanging bead curtain for privacy. She felt so much satisfaction doing that. With a private corner of her own, she wasn't mad or resentful anymore.

LOVE LESSON

1. Where do you feel most like yourself? Is there a corner in the house where you can be alone and do your thing?

2. Be original. Expressing your unique self is oh, so fulfilling. (Your relationship will be fraught with confusion if you don't.) Answer this: What is one thing I enjoy doing that doesn't include anyone else? Try doing that.

3. Explore, seek, and embrace those things that bring you joy and satisfaction. Allow your partner the same opportunity for personal expression. Individual joy will overflow to both of you.

4. Be daring. Everybody has a creative side. Artistic pursuits and projects are extremely helpful for managing stress, coping with loneliness, easing heart- ache, and just making the day a lot more gratifying.

5. Daydream. Studies show that unstructured daydreaming time is an essential component for healthy development of the brains of children. I say it's an essential compo- nent of a balanced, healthy, and happy adult life. Make sure that you aren't booking every moment of your life with a to-do task. Schedule daydreaming time on your calendar to let your mind wander.

WAIT

Lisa has a long list of demands and expectations, and no matter how hard Joe tries, he's seldom able to satisfy her wishes exactly as she wants. For example, Lisa and Joe have an agreement that if she cooks dinner, Joe cleans up. If Joe cooks dinner, Lisa cleans up. Fair exchange, except that Joe prefers to read the paper after dinner. Lisa wants the kitchen cleaned instantly and harps on him to get to it or she begrudgingly does it herself. Occasionally Joe argues back, but mostly he tunes her out and lets her do it.

Jane has a different approach. She plants seeds of suggestion, then cheerfully waits for the seeds to sprout. After 40 years of marriage, she knows the advantage of waiting for events to unfold. Take the hardwood floors as an example. Jane really wanted hardwood floors installed in the entryway and hall, but she knew Greg would need thinking time to see the advantages. With that in mind, she planted a seed of suggestion: "Hardwood floors would spiffy up the entrance and add to the value," she said as she showed him pictures of what she visualized. Then she waited with a smile for his objections.

"They cost too much," he said.

"Yes, hardwoods are expensive," she answered. "Do you think we could find a sale?"

"I think tile is better," he said.

"Tile has advantages," she responded, "but I wonder if tile fits our decor." She gave him a hug, "I really appreciate you thinking about this." Then she let it be.

Jane stated her preferences, she didn't harp or pout. When she did bring up the floors she was pleasant and listened to Greg's point of view. Two years later, Greg woke up one morning and announced, "Let's go look at hardwood floors." That day in the showroom they ordered hardwood floors for the entryway and hall and for the living room as well.

Instinctively Jane knew that there's a higher goal than merely getting your sweetheart to do what you want. By hearing objections she made room for patience. Patience allows us to wait without worry. It is the quality that allows us to encounter disappointment and setbacks with composure. In patience we discover the wonderful things that happen gradually.

LOVE LESSON

1. Look around. Notice the patient folks and the impatient ones. Notice the riled up and the easygoing. Which category are you in?

2. Go easy. Chances are, one of you makes decisions fast and one of you is slower. If that's the case, guess what? You'll both need to cultivate an easygoing style to relate to each other.

3. Notice the gradual. Have you noticed that life unfolds gradually? The more you force, the longer it takes and more goes wrong. The less you force, the quicker things that are meant to be become evident.

4. Plant seeds of suggestion. Continue watering and feeding while you wait for your suggestions to sprout.

5. Simply be. You will contribute to your sweetheart's ease and relaxation as well as your own when you let some things just be.

DO THE RIGHT THING

A five-year-old girl and her three-year-old brother were placed in temporary foster care after the parents were carted off to jail for domestic violence. The frightened little girl was full of questions. "When will I see Mommy and Daddy? When will they come home? Why are they in trouble? Why do they fight?"

"Your mom and dad have to learn to get along," the social worker attempted to explain, "so that you and your brother can go home."

"Where do you go to get along?" the little girl asked. Later she questioned the foster mother, "When will Mom and Dad get along?"

Children raised in a respectful, joy-filled home recognize love when they see it and feel it. Love comes naturally for them. Parents who hurt each other set the stage for more hurt by passing on a legacy of shame and pain. If you are verbally abusive, demanding, distant, critical, self-absorbed, your children will feel fear and inherit shame. There will be a gaping hole in their hearts that they won't know how to heal.

A seven-year-old girl witnessed her drunk mom slap her drunk dad across the face. Dad pushed Mom, who hit her head on the wall. The little girl ran next door and the neighbor called the police, who took Dad to jail and Mom to the emergency room for stitches. The following week Mom brought the little girl for counseling. The little girl didn't want to talk about what happened; instead she drew a picture and told a story. "Once upon a time there was a little girl who picked a flower with her mom and dad."

If your partner is verbally or emotionally abusive, if your partner is an alcoholic or drug addicted, you must do the right thing for yourself and your children. Love is not just words or feelings. Love is doing the right thing. People accuse me of being an optimist and a believer in love, and I admit that it is true. Like the seven-year-old girl, I remain hopeful. Hopeful that people are good and beautiful even when they are trying very hard not to show it. I believe that all of us know what is right action. Right action is often the hardest thing to do, and that is why we sometimes sidestep doing it. A loving relationship cannot be built on attachment alone. Just because you have shared a bed, have kids together, and your finances are entwined, that is not enough to build a loving bond. Healthy relationships lift you up and inspire you to be the best that you can be. A healthy relationship feels good.

LOVE LESSON

1. Always remember: A child is counting on you. If you can't do the right thing for yourself, do it for your children.

2. Heed this warning: Our children's early experiences of love do matter. Love and fear are imprinted on our children's tender minds, hearts, and souls without us noticing.

3. Curb harsh words. Eliminate all abuse. If you are doing and saying things that are hurtful towards your children, seek help immediately. One thing you don't want to fail at is raising your children.

4. Be the best parent you can be. It takes enormous dedication, devotion, loyalty and staunch determination to raise happy, healthy, well-adjusted children. It is a commitment to do everything possible to give them the best start in life.

5. Lead with integrity. Children learn by watching the choices you make and how you live your life. Your duty as a parent has sacred importance. Not only are you teaching your child how to survive in the world, you're teaching how to love others and be a good human being.

SAY MORE WITH LESS

Have you ever noticed that when lovers first come together, they can talk and talk and talk about so many things? They can practically spend the whole night talking with each other, can't they? They can spend hours on the telephone in prized conversations. When you go out to dinner and you look around, you can always spot new lovers because they're looking intently in each other's eyes and talking talking talking talking and smiling smiling smiling. I am keen on watching lovers engaged in love talk.

Talk is a very important part of a love relationship—especially if it is love talk. Love talk is talk that comes from a space of trust and wonder. When my sweetheart, a history buff, was alive he told me all kinds of interesting tidbits. He could weave a story around the Black Death, art, or mathematics that left me weak in the knees and hanging on his words. Fifteen years after his death, I can't recall the details, the dates, or the names of his lectures, but I vividly remember his deep gentle voice, the rhythm of his sentences, and the soothing impact of his breathing.

When Lila lays her head on Carl's shoulder and listens as he explains the appeal of the steam engine, she is transported. Likewise, when Carl hears the enthusiasm in Lila's voice as she shows him the 40th quilt she's working on, he is transfixed. He may not be interested in the patterns but he's engrossed in the sparkle of her eyes, the curve of her fingers as she point to the threads, and the tone of her voice while discussing the patterns. He has heard her descriptions hundreds of times and still he is intrigued.

The way you talk and listen to your sweet one is powerful and has potential to influence the love between you. Do you know the difference between ordinary talk and love talk? Love talk inspires and arouses, lifts each other up, motivates and invigorates, soothes and reassures. Love talk refreshes and energizes the spirit. After such a talk you come alive. Ordinary talk on the other hand is exhausting.

Relationships are doomed when love talk is avoided. The relationships where love can bloom are those where communiqués are filled with wonder. When you can say to your sweetheart, "I am so glad you tell me things, happy things, sad things, frustrating things, truths of all kinds. I am so grateful for the truth between us," love increases.

LOVE LESSON

1. Set the mood. Begin with a smile. Talk gently. Pause. Smile again. Touch. Be friendly. The quality of your message, the softness in your voice, the movement of your body sets the mood for meaningful connected love talk.

2. Speculate. Do not lecture. Talk about what's on your mind, but when you do, say it openly, kindly, gently. Talk in a caring way. Share what's important to you, but don't try to score points to win or talk your loved one into something; none of that will improve your relationship.

3. Marvel. Listen from a space of wonder. Be surprised. Discover something new about your sweetheart and listen this way every day.

4. Connect. Love talk draws you in. If your sweetheart is tuning you out, it may be because you've been jabbering.

5. Lean in. Bend forward. Say less.

CHAPTER X

MOMENTS OF AWAKENING

You fell in love
and your heart
was churned and stirred.
This is an awakening.
Cherish all beautiful
moments of awakening,
for these experiences
point in the direction
of the divine.

LET LOVE TAKE YOU

From the higher-than-the-Eiffel-Tower beginners' love that makes us dizzy and giddy and certain that unseen forces brought us together, to the one-foot-in-front-of-the-other love that keeps us doing the right thing day after day and year after year because that's the commitment we made and the kind of person we are, to the forgiving love that feels like home. Such love recognizes who we are, where we've been, what we've done, and how far we've come, and stays around anyway.

When I began writing this book I heard the word *love* everywhere. "I love cooking," "I love riding my bicycle," "I love movies," "I love shoes," "I love chocolate." At first I was put off by the overuse of "I love," and then I thought, Wonderful. Maybe by giving credit to the ordinary things that bring us pleasure—morning coffee, the sound of rain, a giggling baby, a chirping bird—by seeing beauty around us, perhaps we can expand our admiration for everyday joy. Through tough times and heartaches, through disappointment and despair, love takes us on a journey. We all know life is unfair, but it is still very good. Relationships may not be perfect, but they teach us plenty. According to my friend Dr. Jay, the trick is having the courage to be bad at whatever we are doing long enough to get good at it.

Love motivates us to endure, to rise above our circumstances, to embrace beauty in day-to-day happenings and reach beyond our limitations. Love expands our capacity to open our hearts, to extend ourselves, and be available to what life offers. Through love we find our authentic nature and surprise ourselves.

LOVE LESSON

1. Join. Without love behind our actions we will destroy our families, our community, the planet, and all the creatures that inhabit it. Join other lovers who want the best for everyone and are dedicated to that cause.

2. Strive. As Dr. Jay recommends, "Have the courage to be bad at love long enough to get good at it."

3. Find a love mentor. Turn to a person with integrity, courage, and wisdom. Bow to their guidance.

4. Think *us*. Instead of thinking What is in it for me? think What is in it for us? Every human being—known or unknown to us—and every living creature that crosses our path gives us a chance to respond lovingly. Waiting until it's convenient is not good practice. We are born to love. That's our nature. We are meant to love 24/7. Every chance we get.

5. Begin. This is the time for love. This moment. Right now. Today. Repeat out loud: "I wouldn't want a day without love in it." Let go of ideas of what love ought to have been or what love should be and take hold of love as it is.

COMMUNE WITH HIGHER WISDOM

Being a lover and a seeker of all things love is similar to being a gardener. When you work in a garden, you are in touch with the unseen force behind all life. As outside distractions melt away you feel connected to that divine energy. We frequently are so caught up in minuscule issues that we forget about how we are connected to the higher wisdom that makes life and love possible.

My grandmother was a gardener. She said there was joy in the harvest, and that's wonderful and exciting, and she also explained that gardening requires diligence and respect for the whole process—and in a way that's even more satisfying. A gardener doesn't have control over the weather. If there isn't enough water available or there isn't enough sun, there's nothing you can do. In some cities there are times when you're not allowed to water your lawn because of water shortages. And in other parts of the world, things are much, much worse. So in the face of something like a water shortage, the only thing to do is turn to a higher power and ask for help.

Now, I am not trying to talk to you about religion. I do not want to lay a trip on you. I am not trying to talk you into believing in God if you don't. When I use the word *God*, I mean there is a much higher wisdom in the universe than mere human intelligence—a much higher wisdom and a much higher love—and that we are intimately connected with this higher love-wisdom. Some people can't see any beauty in people. Those same people treat their own families terribly. They can't see any beauty in the human spirit. If you can't see the beauty in the human spirit, you can't see God.

Look at it this way. It is enough for us to plant a seed and care for it, but we can't actually make it grow. A seed grows because of an unseen force in the universe, and this unseen force is the energy behind all life. When we plant the seed, we know there is a divine force that will make the seed grow. That's the miracle of life. The seed doesn't even have to struggle.

We struggle much more than we need to. This is true regarding just about everything. Once we ask a higher power for help, it all becomes much easier. I was very young and I loved it when my grandmother talked to me about gardening. She had grown blind, but still she had one of the most beautiful gardens I ever saw. Being blind didn't stop her one bit.

LOVE LESSON

1. Turn to a higher power. Ask this higher wisdom to run the show and to guide you.

2. Let go. You can't do it all. This world is so complex, there are so many uncertainties, so many unforeseeable pitfalls—not only for us but for our loved ones, too. Pick up any newspaper. As you read about all the terrible things that are happening, you almost feel your heart is going to break.

3. Ask for inner peace. Trust. Wait. Trust. Believe. A higher love is working on your behalf.

4. Plant a garden. A garden is a reminder that God is everywhere. Your garden can be a few herbs in a pot or a community pea patch. Commune with the power of the unseen force.

5. Fixate on beauty. Look for beauty in gardens and in the human spirit. The beauty you see is a reflection of your own.

THANK YOUR LUCKY STARS

A love relationship is more than we imagine it to be—more than romance, more than a living arrangement, more than a work and play cooperative. When spirits connect, a sacred mission is placed in motion. Such a spiritual alliance adds another dimension to a relationship, one more subtle. You can sense it forming but you cannot see it; it is invisible.

Satya and Jonah refer to each other as soul mates. When they first met they clicked instantly, were drawn together as if they'd known each other before. Right off the bat they could talk about anything, they had so much to share. People say they are the perfect match not because they do not have challenges or setbacks, but because they address hurdles and conflicts from a broader perspective. Satya and Jonah hold a similar perspective about what genuine love offers.

What is genuine, bona fide love? Well, it is not needy, clingy, grabby, demanding, deprived, depressed, withdrawn, tight, or fearful, and it is not the opposite of these attributes either. After all, even the most loving among us experience painful feelings and dark thoughts. Negative attributes are part of us, but those attributes are not our entire nature. When folks get stuck believing the worst they operate from a dark unconscious stance. Soul mates understand the tendency to judge harshly, so they commit to helping each other climb out of the muck. They recognize that we are not who we think we are, not who others think we are—we are much, much more.

Soul mates value truth that is larger than observable reality, beyond what they immediately recognize. They strive to be open about inner struggles. They make every effort to examine their own psyches, and that endeavor keeps them grounded in the spiritual reality that their birthright is joy and happiness. When life feels like drudgery, when relationships fall flat, when challenges seem insurmountable, soul mates remind each other that all is divine and they thank their lucky stars.

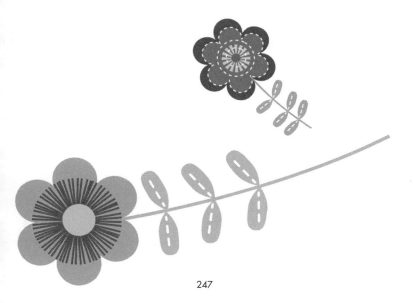

LOVE LESSON

1. Strengthen your alliance. What views about spirituality do you share? Do you share mystical identity, a joint vision? What is your spiritual intention? Surround yourself with couples who are considering these questions too.

2. Thank your lucky stars. Some relationships feel deeper than others. If you have a spiritual bond, you are very lucky.

3. Rely on a spiritual alliance. When you're down in the dumps, turn to your mate and allow him or her to guide you and lift you up. Do this for each other. A spiritual alliance is stronger and wiser than any other.

4. Stay on course. There is a purpose to your relationship that is bigger than paying the bills and keeping food on the table. You are together to remind each other that all is divine. Say, "Honey there's a spiritual purpose for being together."

5. Love unconditionally. Soul mates lift each other up. They want the best for each other. Such a relationship is not based on competition or ego but on rising above dark unconscious tendencies so that each can be all that he or she is meant to be. Rejoice in that undertaking.

ACCOMPANY YOUR SWEETIE

Paul accompanied Margo to the cancer care clinic for her weekly chemo. She was exhausted after treatment and the thought of driving 45 minutes home alone was horrendous. Without her saying a word about what she was dreading and before she could ask for his help, Paul stepped up and said, "I am going with you." He went along to every doctor's appointment, every procedure, and every treatment. He wanted to; it wasn't an imposition. He knew this wasn't fun for her and he wanted to give her support, to nurture her, to be by her side. He felt helpless to make the cancer go away—which he would have if he could have—so he did the only thing he could do and that was to be there for her, to drive the car and provide a calming presence. Margo felt guilty at times that Paul was going through this with her. She wished he could be doing something fun, but it meant everything to her that he was so willing to join her.

Seeing what your partner needs, stepping up and giving it without your partner asking, is an offering of compassion. When you notice that what your partner needs is your presence alongside, when you accompany your partner without complaining, you both are enriched by such a simple contribution.

LOVE LESSON

1. Accompany your sweetheart. When your honeybunch is nervous about going alone, go along. Even if it is only a tiny errand that makes your sweetie anxious, drop what you are doing and go. Sometimes we have to go places we don't want to go. Your sweetheart can drive you to the dentist, sit in the waiting room with you, even buy you a milkshake afterward, but you have to sit in the chair all alone. On such occasions it sure is a wonderful bonus to have a sweet one waiting for you.

2. Step up. See what your sweetheart needs and do it. When a loved one is under pressure, facing a difficult situation, or overwhelmed, he may not know what is needed or be able to ask for what he would like. In those situations, look around, see what your partner might need. Give him that.

3. Send reassuring glances. Each time you give a reassuring glance you send a comforting message. Each time you are by your sweetheart's side you make her day a little brighter.

4. Ask, "Honey, may I go with you?" If your honey says, "No, I can go by myself," say, "I know you can, but this time I'd like to be by your side."

5. Give. Often it is the tiniest act that is so helpful. Accompanying your sweetheart is not something you have to do, it is something you decide to give, and that act of kindness is contagious.

WALK ON THE CHEERY SIDE

There are significant issues that require a thoughtful response, but still it's possible to see those issues through a lighthearted lens. The trick is to know the difference between what will matter an hour from now, a year from now, and what will not. Most of the time it's how you handle the issues that determines whether or not the discussion takes a nosedive and turns contentious. It's not only solving problems that forms deep bonds, it's being able to laugh as you muddle through them. What it all boils down to is this: If you can't make each other laugh you are not going to make it. It's laughing and getting a kick out of our eccentricities that wards off weightiness. Lovers really can be silly. Swooning, calling each other love names, giggling, touching, smiling, hanging on every word, being amused, whispering sweet nothings. The more difficult your predicament, the more you will need to lighten the atmosphere with an amiable viewpoint.

Jack is good at sweet nothings. That's what Ana told me when I asked her how they've kept the fires burning after 22 years. "Hasn't always been easy," she said, and gave me a wonderful example. In the car on the way to a company party they had a doozy of a fight. She can't remember what the fight was about but she remembers being so furious that she threatened to take a cab home. In the middle of the party Jack came up behind her and whispered in her ear, "You're a feisty one and I like it." He had such a twinkle in his eye that she couldn't stay mad for long. Given an opportunity, she'll seduce him with a discreet game of footsies or snuggle up beside him and tell him how handsome he looks. Jack gets a kick out of it too.

Lovers are so cheery. It's as if a bubble of positive energy surrounds them, rendering them good-natured. Hanging around them, you're either delighted to see what's possible or envious because you're craving positive energy for yourself.

LOVE LESSON

1. Look on the cheerful side. If you are always serious, you're moving into a danger zone and at risk of becoming uptight, grim, staid, and somber. Discover humor in inconveniences. Okay, so he washed his black socks with the white guest towels again. Is this a tragedy? Is it really a calamity that she keeps you waiting 15 minutes almost every time?

2. Think of it this way: Serious issues are the issues that your partner considers serious, and nonserious issues are yours. Get it? Okay, that's a joke. The point is that most serious issues can be approached with a witty, upbeat perspective.

3. Be a fool. Have you ever made of fool of yourself for love? Well, I hope so. If not, then you are avoiding.

4. Evaluate. Will this matter in an hour, tomorrow, next week, next year? Ten years from now?

5. Take a lesson from the stern ones. Some folks are squeamish about being playful. If you ask a strict pair why they're no longer in love, they will supply you with a list of shortcomings. Not their own shortcomings but their partner's shortcomings. (The partner is at fault. Blame is the game. Point the finger. Not my fault. Yours. You. You, over there, are the sole reason for the demise of romance.) I suggest you don't do that.

WELCOME JOY

If you have ever jumped out of bed excited about the ordinary day, if you still get a thrill hearing your sweetheart's voice, if you sometimes feel a wave of happiness for no apparent reason other than that you are still breathing, that is an indication you are ready for joy. Joy is the attitude that it is good to be alive. We have what we need, and that fills us up. There is nothing—I repeat: nothing—as important as everyday love. If we respond to beauty in the everyday acts of kindness, the beauty of a face, the beauty of a wild creature roaming freely in its habitat, we are experiencing joy. Joy really does depend on where we put our attention. Day-to-day life, with its trials and tribulations, with it's victories and delights, with all its contradictions, is where love grows, where kindness abounds, where joy is found.

At first glance, Allison and Brad seem to be a maze of contradictions. Allison is an outgoing fast talker with an enormous circle of friends. She likes being involved in the community and raises money for all kinds of events from the symphony to the animal shelter. She buys stylish clothes at consignment stores and text-messages her adult children many times a day. Brad, her husband of 42 years, is a loner, an absent-minded intellectual content with reading and listening to music on headphones. He walks his dog, grows tomatoes, and lies in a hammock. He wears the same green wool sweater every single day except Valentine's Day and Christmas, when he wears a red one, or in the summer, when it is too hot and he wears a wrinkled cotton shirt. When I asked them the secret to their long-lasting relationship, she answered, "What's not to love?" Brad nodded in agreement.

There is so much bliss in day-to-day life. An enlightened relationship is based on joy. Being alive and loving is the prime concern in such a union. When two people are able to let go of the false premise that ordinary life and love are separate, they find bliss ever present. When there is inner peace and contentment in ordinary day-to-day life, life is not ordinary at all.

LOVE LESSON

1. Be grateful. If you woke up this morning and heard birds singing, be thankful for another day. Gather all the moments of beauty, for these are the moments of prayer.

2. Welcome joy. Have you thought about joy? Have you imagined a day filled with joy? How is joy expressed in your home? How much joy will you allow? Joy is a reflection of the soul, a subtle harmony of body, mind, and spirit. Joy is our nature.

3. Speak highly of your beloved ones. Always! Never make a mean-spirited comment (even in jest) about your partner, your children, your friends—even if they aren't around. This is one of the quickest ways to ruin a day.

4. Let go of the idea that daily life and love are separate. Look for beauty every day. Take love in. Speak of joy. Let others know that you are glad to be alive.

5. Be a mentor of joy. When you find joy in ordinary days, ordinary days are not ordinary at all. Celebrate being alive and you will be in love with life.

NOTICE THE NOTHING

Love is not meant to be reserved for the right person, the right moment, the perfect setting, or the ideal mood—love is the condition of your heart. You can love your mom, your dad, your grandma, the moon, birds, the sky, children, trees, neighbors, strangers. There are so many things on this planet to love. Have you noticed dewdrops on a flower petal? Have you felt raindrops on your skin? Have you stood still to take a closer look at the colors that make up a sunset? Have you fallen in love with waves in the ocean? Have you been head over heels in love with morning light? Have you seen the spark in your sweetheart's eyes? Been enamored by giggles? Been moved to tears?

Unless you love those things, you cannot love at all. If you've been too hasty to notice clouds, too preoccupied to be grateful for another day, too busy to press your lips together and share breath with your sweetheart, when will you love? A hurried-up style is anti-love. Love is heart-felt participation in the miracle of being alive. Or as a gentleman on my bird-watching hike put it, "If you don't love the birds, you won't notice the curves."

It's easy to acknowledge a surprise grand gesture offered out of the blue, but much harder to appreciate ordinary behavior performed routinely in the midst of the daily grind. If you wait for your honey to do something special before showing appreciation, you'll be missing a major opportunity to strengthen your connection and deepen your love.

LOVE LESSON

1. Notice the nothing. Meaningful, life-changing appreciation begins at the most basic of levels. Appreciate the tiniest "nothings," such as the traits that are a natural part of your sweetheart's character, and the things that you have come to expect and value and would miss if they were gone.

2. Love now, not just on rare occasions. Go out of your way to be kind to everyone and everything you encounter—friends, family, neighbors, strangers, birds, worms, trees, blades of grass, people on computers, people on cell phones, people on bicycles, rocks, shirts, shoes, teeth, toes, elbows. Even the smallest displays of love have a way of spreading quickly and widely.

3. Approach your sweetheart as if you have everything to learn, as if you know nothing. In fact it is true that we know nearly nothing. There is so much more to learn about each other.

4. Search for meaning. Every relationship has meaning that is higher than being together. What is the spiritual purpose of your relationship?

5. Act in friendliness. The day shrinks or expands in proportion to the love you recognize, accept, and give. Let love shine through all of your actions. Hang out with happy couples and kind people. Be of good cheer.

ABOUT THE AUTHOR

Judy Ford, a trained professional psychotherapist with heart, soul, and life experience, is the author of the award-winning *Wonderful Ways to Love a Child* and *Single: The Art of Being Satisfied, Fulfilled and Independent*. Articles on her work have appeared in *O: The Oprah Magazine*, *Family Circle*, *Woman's World*, *Cosmopolitan*, *Woman's Day*, and *Glamour*, among others. Her media appearances include *Oprah*, CNN, and National Public Radio. She lives in Kirkland, Washington, where she maintains a psychotherapy practice and keeps a regular speaking schedule. She has been studying love and relationships for over three decades, specializing in love, loss, and the things that matter most. She is passionate about riding her electric bicycle and creating papier-mâché bracelets. Visit her online at www.judyford.com.

TO OUR READERS

Viva Editions publishes books that inform, enlighten, and entertain. We do our best to bring you, the reader, quality books that celebrate life, inspire the mind, revive the spirit, and enhance lives all around. Our authors are practical visionaries: people who offer deep wisdom in a hopeful and helpful manner. Viva was launched with an attitude of growth and we want to spread our joy and offer our support and advice where we can to help you live the Viva way: vivaciously!

We're grateful for all our readers and want to keep bringing you books for inspired living. We invite you to write to us with your comments and suggestions, and what you'd like to see more of. You can also sign up for our online newsletter to learn about new titles, author events, and special offers.

Viva Editions
2246 Sixth St.
Berkeley, CA 94710
www.vivaeditions.com
(800) 780-2279
Follow us on Twitter @vivaeditions
Friend/fan us on Facebook